LAND, AGRICULTURE AND INDUSTRY IN NORTH-WEST ESSEX

Spotlights on a land remembered

SWHS PUBLICATIONS

LAND, AGRICULTURE AND INDUSTRY IN NORTH-WEST ESSEX

Spotlights on a land remembered

Geoffrey Ball

SWHS Publications

SERIES EDITOR JACQUELINE COOPER

Other publications by Saffron Walden Historical Society:

Ward, Jennifer C., *The De Bohun Charter of Saffron Walden* (1986)

Saffron Walden History (Journal: 1972-1991)

Saffron Walden Historical Journal (2001-)

ISBN 978-1-873669-02-0

Published by SWHS Publications

Hon. Editor: 24 Pelham Road, Clavering, Essex CB11 4PQ, England.

Contents

List of Illustrations

Cover Picture: *Ploughing* by Sir George Clausen, R.A. (1852-1944), oil painting 1889. Reproduced by kind permission of Aberdeen Art Gallery, and the Copyright Trustee of the Clausen family.
Frontispiece: Map of North-west Essex, showing places mentioned in text.

25. Milking and salving sheep *circa* 1340, from Backhouse, J., *Medieval Rural Life in the Luttrell Psalter* (The British Library, 2000), p.30. Illustration by permission of The British Library: Add.42130f.163v.

26. Medieval sheepcote. Illustration from Hartley, D. & Elliot, M., *Life & Work of the People of England* (Batsford, 1931).

27. Modern Tenter Frame. Illustration from Aspin, C., *The Woollen Industry* (Shire Publications, 1982). Reproduced by permission of Chris Aspin and Shire Publications.

28: Woolstaplers' Hall, Saffron Walden. Illustration by courtesy of Saffron Walden Town Library.

29. Carved heads in Woolstaplers' Hall, Saffron Walden. Illustration by courtesy of Saffron Walden Town Library.

30. Reconstruction of how the Castle Hill site may have looked in medieval times. Illustration from Cromarty, D. 'Chepyng Walden 1381-1420: a study from the Court Rolls' in *Essex Journal* II (1967), p. 106. Reproduced by courtesy of the family of the late Dorothy Cromarty.

31. Reconstruction of Saffron Walden town layout in 1400. Illustration from Cromarty, D. 'Chepyng Walden 1381-1420: a study from the Court Rolls' in *Essex Journal* II (1967), p. 106. As Ill.30. Reproduced by courtesy of the family of the late Dorothy Cromarty.

32 & 33. Cards and a wool comb. Reproduced by courtesy of Norfolk Museums & Archaeology Service.

34. Combing, carding and spinning. Illustration from Hartley, D. & Elliot, M., *Life and Work of the People of England* (Batsford, 1931).

35. Ram's head carving. Illustration by Donald Stewart, reproduced with permission from Everett, M., & Stewart, D., *The Buildings of Saffron Walden* (Harts, 2004).

36. Norfolk ewe and Southdown cross lamb. Hand-coloured lithograph based on a painting by William Shiels. Illustration from Wade-Martins, P., *Black Faces: a history of East Anglian Sheep Breeds* (Norfolk Museums Service, 1993). Reproduced by courtesy of author and Norfolk Museum Service.

37. Bishop Blaize, from a West Country trade token. Illustration from *Littlebury: A Parish History* (2005), p.74 by kind permission of The Parish of Littlebury Millennium Society History Group.

38. Bishop Blaize, the Spring family parclose in the parish church of St Peter & St Paul, Lavenham. Photograph Margaret Ashton.

39. Processes of woollen and worsted industries. Illustration from Lipson, E., *A History of the English Woollen and Worsted Industries* (1921).

40. The last day of Saffron Walden cattle market in 1981. Photographs ©Gordon Ridgewell.

41. Steam threshing at Ashdon 1924. Photograph ©Gordon Ridgewell.

Editor's Preface

This volume is the first in a new series of local history books, the SWHS Publications. This series is sponsored by the Saffron Walden Historical Society, publishers of the *Saffron Walden Historical Journal*. In common with the *Journal*, SWHS Publications aims to bring into the public domain works of original research which are worthy of wider readership, and which relate to the history of North-west Essex. Each volume will be a quality production, but modestly priced with a limited print run, and non-profitmaking, with all income going towards future publications. We hope by this means to add to published material on the history of this area, either from the fruits of new research, or to bring to light other works of history long out-of-print and worthy of reproduction.

The Author

Born in France in 1926, Geoffrey Ball acquired an interest in agriculture when recruited, during the war, to help gather in the vital potato crop. After childhood in London, aged 18 he joined the Parachute Regiment and served in Palestine at the end of the British Mandate, where he was able to witness the development of Israeli agriculture before the establishment of the state of Israel. Back in England he spent a year working with the leading English herd of Ayshire cattle, following this with a course in agriculture at Lackham College, Wiltshire. There followed several years gaining further experience and an introduction to markets and sheep fairs in Wiltshire and adjoining counties. In 1954 Geoffrey moved abroad to take up a new life in Central Africa, working for the Northern Rhodesia government to improve African agriculture. When in 1967, Northern Rhodesia had metamorphosed into Zambia, he returned to England and took up a sales and advisory post with Fisons Fertilisers, which brought him into contact with the farming community all over North Essex. In 1977 Geoffrey moved to Pertwee Holdings Ltd (agricultural merchants, fertiliser manufacturers and contractors), ending his career 11 years later as Sales and Marketing Director responsible for a wide area of East Anglia. After living in Wimbish for 20 years, Geoffrey moved to Saffron Walden in 1996, where he has become interested in studying and writing about the history of the industry in which he once worked. The author thus brings a lifetime's knowledge and experience to this published study of farming and its associated industries in a very special part of Essex.

Jacqueline Cooper
Hon. Editor, SWHS Publications

Foreword

Geoffrey Ball's book has its origins in a series of individual articles first published in the *Saffron Walden Historical Journal*.* Published together they provide a fascinating exploration of the agricultural history of North-west Essex, and the agriculturally based industries that were the source of the area's prosperity over several centuries.

It is tempting to think of Saffron Walden as an isolated, self-sufficient rural community, but this is far from the truth, as the town and the surrounding area was increasingly drawn into the market based economies created by the growth of large urban centres such as London and Cambridge. As early as the end of the 14th century Saffron Walden had become an important market for the trading of grain, malt and occasionally large consignments of wool.

Industries such as malting and weaving not only provided people with a source of income, they also transformed the physical appearance of the town, resulting in the construction of specialised buildings, such as the many maltings, with 'their cowls rising up in all directions'. Weaving has also left its mark on the fabric of the town. The timber-framing inside many picturesque cottages still bears the scars from wooden looms worked centuries ago. The final, short-lived revival in the early 19th century, when there were as many as 900 looms in Walden and the surrounding villages, resulted in the construction of rows of tiny cottages in East Street, Mount Pleasant and at Copt Hall in Ashdon Road.

The way land was owned and worked, the crops that were planted, the form taken by animal husbandry and the technology used, created a way of life that shaped the countryside and the towns. It helps to explain vast disparities of wealth, and the periodic rebellion of the people who created that wealth but owned nothing. Work and the life of the community were tuned to the seasons and the rhythms of sowing and harvesting. The unhurried pace of Geoffrey Ball's gentle and persuasive prose provides the perfect introduction to that vanished way of life and the legacy it has left us.

Martyn Everett

*The original articles can be found in *Saffron Walden Historical Journal* issue numbers 2, 3, 4, 5, 7, 8, 9, 12, 13 and 14 (2001-2007).

Acknowledgements

I wish to thank the following people for their help in the preparation of this book: Martyn Everett, former Local Studies Librarian, Saffron Walden Town Library for invaluable help in finding sources amongst the Town Library books and maps collection. The staff of the Bishops Stortford Museum for access to books in their collection. Laurie Barker, London, for general information and notes on malting in Saffron Walden. Zofia Everett for general help with records kept at the ERO Archive Access Point, Saffron Walden. Gordon Ridgewell for reproducing several photographs prior to publication. Elisabeth Barrett of the Ware Museum for help with illustrations and permission to use the diagram of malting processes. Shirley Miller and Julia Bazley at Saffron Walden Museum. Gillian Williamson and Lizzie Sanders for access to records for Littlebury. The Jersey Cattle Society of the United Kingdom and the Royal Jersey Agricultural and Horticultural Society for information concerning the history of Jersey cattle and the Audley End Jerseys in particular. The late Mrs Carol Tinney, wife of the present farmer and owner of Mitchells, for access to her research notes on Mitchells Farm. Graham Taylor of Greencore Malting Group. Also to acknowledge the help of all staff in the Saffron Walden Library on many occasions. I would like to thank Lizzie Sanders for her great expertise in designing the book cover. Finally, without the help in the preparation for publication of Jacqueline Cooper, the book may have never seen the light of day. Therefore I would like to express my thanks to her also for unstinting support and encouragement at all times.

Geoffrey Ball
April 2009

Cover picture: 'Ploughing' by Sir George Clausen RA (1852-1944), oil painting 1889. Reproduced by kind permission of Aberdeen Art Gallery, and the Copyright Trustee of the Clausen family. Sir George Clausen lived at Widdington and Duton Hill. Much of his work depicts the rigours of winter work on farms, faithfully portraying rural realism. This painting is something of an anachronism since, by 1889, wooden ploughs had been superseded by iron ploughs, which were first recorded at Manningtree, Essex in 1773.

Introduction

Agriculture and its associated industries have been at the centre of life and work in north-west Essex over many centuries. In an area devoid of other natural resources, agricultural production, marketing and processing have supplied not only food products but they have been a major source of employment. It is this theme which runs through the seven contributions to local history encompassed in this volume.

Four of them focus on local farming history of different types and at varying historical periods. Agricultural practices have never been static – change, improvement and new ideas mostly leading to enhanced productivity have been a constant feature. Before the arrival of science into the world of agrarian activities during the 19th century, change was brought about by leading, innovative farmers responding to new ideas and market conditions of the time.

The first chapter looks at a local example of common field (or open field) farming close to Saffron Walden. Although one of the earliest forms of English farming, it persisted in NW Essex, but on an ever decreasing scale, until its final removal in the 19th century by Parliamentary and Private Enclosure Acts. At that time new individual tenanted farms were created having all their land enclosed and a set of farm buildings provided by the landlord.

The three chapters which follow examine three very different local farms, two from the 19th century and the third a long and detailed history of a typical north Essex holding located on the difficult heavy clay soil at Little Walden.

In the remaining chapters the focus changes somewhat to industries directly connected with the products of farming which at different periods in local history have been important to the success of Saffron Walden and its environs.

Malting barley for beers and ales has been a major contributor to the wealth of the area with over 30 maltings in operation at one time and 80 per cent of the malt carried to London. Sadly to see the town today one has to look very hard indeed to find any evidence on the ground. The few remaining buildings have been put to other uses in redevelopment schemes.

A 19th century outline plan to construct a canal into and past Saffron Walden is the subject of the next chapter. The malting industry had always been hampered by the excessive cost of road transport to London or later to Bishop's Stortford, the canal terminal for London via Ware in Hertfordshire. Several previous attempts had been made to extend the canal from Bishop's Stortford to Saffron Walden and beyond but all had proved fruitless. As with previous plans this too failed to gain acceptance and the benefits to the malting industry were never realised.

The long history of the local wool industry is the subject of the final three-part chapter. Sheep were vital to local farming and were part and parcel of the predominately arable system. The wool they produced provided employment for large numbers of people engaged in hand spinning and other processes connected with the preparation and marketing of wool before the expansion of the malting industry.

Over the past 40 years North-west Essex and Saffron Walden town especially have witnessed many changes resulting in a lower profile for local farming. These changes are reviewed in the Postscript, together with some thoughts and concerns about the importance of agriculture in our national life.

Geoffrey Ball

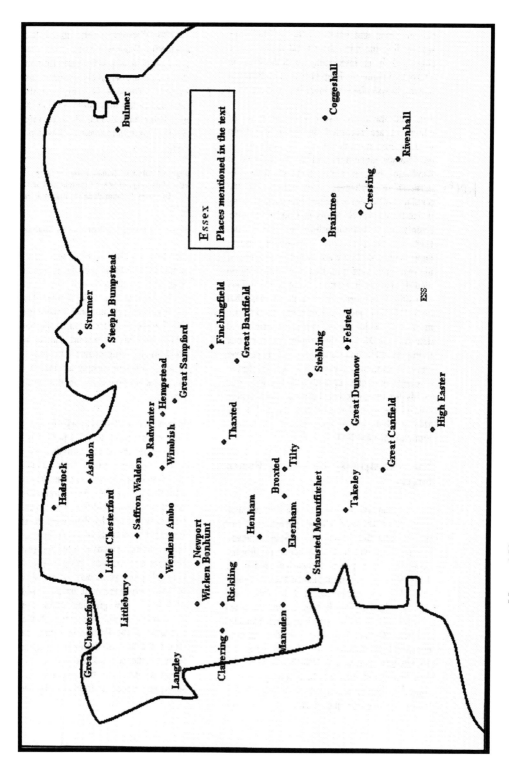

Map of North-west Essex showing places mentioned in the text.

1

Local farming in a bygone age: what was it like?

The long history of Saffron Walden as a marketing centre arises from its inseparable contact with the land of the surrounding country. Industries that thrived were nearly all closely connected with marketing and processing agricultural products. A few examples that come to mind are saffron, wool, barley and malt, wheat and flour, livestock and meat, dairy products especially cheese and butter, hides and leather and so on. What was the farming like that produced this range of products, how was it organised, and who held the land in the centuries before the 19th century when enclosure finally brought about the demise of a centuries-old way of life? What follows will, I hope, provide some answers to these questions.

To cast some light on the subject of who held the land and its use in former times, it is necessary to look back to the Middle Ages when in principle all land belonged to the Crown. Manorial lords held land directly from the King in return for services, and these lords in turn had people holding land from them, again in return for services. The types of services varied and were defined by the tenure under which the land was held. Most land today is subject to private property rights but this was not so in the Middle Ages when much land was subject to common property rights and customary law whereby the right of ownership did not give exclusive right of use. Although an individual owned land, other people living in the community had the right to use that land in various ways, for example arable farming, grazing, fuel and settlement. Most of those using the land in these ways were customary tenants and subject to customary law administered by their manor court.

In the immediate vicinity of Saffron Walden there were two manors, Brook Walden and Chipping Walden. A Steward of the Manor was the senior figure and he would have been largely responsible for agrarian matters.[1] The manor court was the body through which the lord administered his responsibilities for agrarian management and control. An example of the sort of control exercised would be a tenant who held land 'at the will of the lord' and therefore, according to the custom of the manor, was thereby subject to customary law. If he wished to transfer his holding of land to another person, for example father to son, the transaction had to be recorded in the manor court roll. The tenant received a copy of the entry which in time became known as copyhold. While this was not a free tenure it was heritable and gave a significant measure of security. However, if the copyholder wished to transfer his land, as suggested above, the manor court could demand an entry fine from the incoming tenant. A similar fine could be applied if the holder of the land died and his heirs wished to sell the copyhold. This was in effect a fee charged to enter the property. Not all tenants held land by 'copy' but only 'at will'. This tenure was of lower status and gave little security. Most of the services required from these 'unfree' customary tenants were largely commuted to money payments as time went on.

The tenants of the manor lived in crofts and farmed in the 'open fields' — a term used by modern historians — which were located locally to the north and south of Saffron Walden and, to a lesser extent, to the east of the town (Figure 1). Predominantly, but not exclusively, they farmed the lighter chalky soils which were in the areas of earliest settlement. To the west of Walden there was demesne land which by 1561 was the property of the 1st Earl of Suffolk, owner of the Audley End Estate. In earlier times some of this land had been open fields, part of Walden Abbey. These tenant farmers were first and foremost subsistence cultivators who sold produce, mainly grain, if it was surplus to family requirements. The family grain requirements were obtained from about 2¼ acres of land per person on a three-field system so a family of five would require a minimum of 11¼ acres for subsistence alone.[2] It has been estimated that about 80% of farmers in England were probably living at subsistence level at the start of the 16th century and a high percentage of holdings in north-west Essex were less than 20 acres in extent. However, locally the percentage of subsistence farmers may well have been less as this was an area well suited to cereal growing where yields would have been higher than the national average and could have produced more frequently a surplus for the market. Unfortunately peasant farmers kept no records.

Fig 1. The straight lines running down from right to left in this picture indicate some of the remnants of strip cultivation in Birdbush Field, Saffron Walden, between Newport Road and Debden Road, near to what is now Rowntree Way. The strips clearly relate to those shown on the 1758 map of Audley End Farm. The girls pictured are standing on the grass baulks which divided each strip. The photograph is dated c.1912.

The next point to consider is their method of farming – the cows and ploughs part. Firstly, it was essentially a cooperative system where the fields in which they farmed contained land held by many tenant farmers. These open fields were divided into shotts and each farmer had his own strips of land within the shott that had been allocated to him by the manor for his use. The strips were sometimes 220 yards long, the distance a team of oxen were said to be able to plough without a rest and known as a furlong (see Fig. 1). The width of the strip could be 22 yards making an acre in total. These strips often became an elongated 'S' shape as the oxen used for ploughing started to turn before the end of the furrow. Four oxen and a plough was roughly 40 feet in length so a large turning circle was necessary. The teams of oxen were usually owned jointly by several co-operating farmers and the plough may also have been jointly owned by the same group.

A rotation of crops was followed by all the farmers having land in any one field, wheat being sown in the autumn and barley in the spring, these being the two cereal crops everyone grew. In addition to the two fields being cropped there was a third – 'the three-field system' mentioned earlier – which was fallowed or rested for a year from cropping. This field was used from harvest onwards for grazing, thus benefiting from the replacement of some plant nutrients by the grazing animal, until the time arrived to plough for the next crop when the rotation would begin again. Wheat was the first crop after fallow. All farmers had land in at least three fields but many had similar strips in yet more fields often far distant from their homestead.

The problems arising from small fragmented arable strips was a serious impediment to progressive farming and resulted in much lost time at critical periods. Field drainage was hindered by multiple occupation and a mass of field paths. Significant increases in yields were almost impossible to achieve for many reasons and compared unfavourably with enclosed land, about which more later. Average grain yields in the medieval period are always difficult to gauge but 10 to 11 bushels of barley per acre can be used for an average crop with rather less for wheat and oats. Of this gross yield, two to three bushels would have to be retained for tithe and seed for the following year. Cereal yields were slow to advance but by the mid-16th century the average was about 13 to 14 bushels per acre. According to some figures from Norfolk, significant increases in yield only came about after 1750 and then continued to rise quite steeply into the 19th century. By 1850 barley yields had advanced to about 40 bushels per acre by which time soil fertility levels were much higher than they had been in the era of the open fields.

While numerically the largest group of farmers were these customary tenants holding open field land, there were also seven large leasehold farms within the two manors. These seven were what we would recognise today as farms complete with a farmhouse, set of buildings and fields - known as 'closes' which were demarcated by hedges in contrast to the open fields outside their boundaries. All seven were part of the Audley End Estate and leased by individual tenants able to farm large acreages. These farms ranged in size from 56 acres to over 300 acres and as time went on incorporated additional land gained from purchases and exchanges of open field strips. The farm maps of 1758 show these farms together with contiguous areas of open fields.[3] Their names were St Aylotts, Butlers, Westley, Ross, Pounce Hall, Monks Hall and Audley End Farm. Apart from Pounces, all the others remain as working farms to this day. Nearly all are located near the 300 foot contour at which level the soils generally become heavier and naturally less free-draining than the soils at lower levels, but have greater potential for higher yields and were thus favoured by those able to undertake the extra cost of farming heavy land.

Rentals reflected the difference in value between open field lands in north-west Essex at 7s to 10s per acre whereas enclosed land was valued at 15s to 20s per acre according to Arthur Young, writing in 1807.[4] Most of the original farmhouses had been replaced in the 16th and 17th centuries by the structures which stand today but often with alterations and additions. Apart from the houses, a range of conveniently located buildings would have been provided for the farmer which were maintained jointly by landlord and tenant.

In 1747, just prior to the partition of the Audley End Estate, a survey was carried out of these seven leasehold farms in Brook and Chipping Walden, as well as other farms in the manors which were subsequently granted to Lord Hervey under the terms of the partition of 1753. At that time several of the farms were in a poor state and concern was expressed about retaining tenants or finding replacements. One of the greatest problems for landlords in managing these large commercial farms was finding and retaining enterprising tenants who were capable of making sufficient profit not only to pay the rent, but to have access to the capital to finance their farming operations. An example of the concern expressed is as follows: 'paling, hedges, ditches, gates, bridges, stiles in the worst condition I ever saw. It is absolutely necessary therefore to put it in tolerable order that some profit might arise and that who ever came to look on it might not be frightened or give it an ill character'.[5] Again, 'Rent had been raised a few years since nine pounds yearly which is abated to the New Tenant and his bargain is dear enough. The house is ready to fall, ye roof must be taken off and thorough repaired this spring', etc. etc.[6] Generally the farms in the outlying manors were in poorer condition than those in Brook or Chipping Walden.

Arthur Young detailed the costs involved in setting up a farm, presumably of 100 acres as he began with a requirement of five horses at £30 each. At the time it was considered usual that five or six horses were required per 100 acres. What he terms as the 'Principal Items' amounted to £1,548, a considerable sum which only a very few could be expected to raise. The list includes the livestock, necessary not only for the market, but also to maintain the fertility of the fields. The grazing animal and farm yard manure were realistically the only available sources of plant nutrients apart from legumes such as clover, beans or sainfoin. Mixed farming was essential if soil fertility was to be maintained. Most of these farms had both sheep and cattle.

In order to ensure that soil fertility was not put at risk, strict compliance by the tenant was required who had to agree to a limit on the number of cereal crops in the rotation. Normally on the heavier land, where turnips were not grown for fodder, the rotation would still include a bare fallow to clean the ground. At most, two cereal crops in four years separated by a legume such as peas or beans were grown. On the lighter land turnips were grown which were either fed off in the field, or carried off for yarded stock and were regarded as a cleaning crop, when grown in rows that could be hoed.

Before leaving the subject of those who held land, reference should be made to the freehold farms, several of which became part of Audley End estate as a result of purchases during the second half of the 18th century, but by no means all. A number remained as freehold properties into the 20th century. The Saffron Walden Enclosure Award of 1823 finally terminated open field agriculture in the parish and the land was allocated to various landowners. A few new farms were set up, on former open field land and the pattern set for a totally commercial agriculture capable of producing the additional food for a rising population but not without social disturbance and hardship for many people.

2

The Victorian Home Farm at Audley End

Any visit to Audley End House, park and garden is likely to include some time spent looking at the Victorian Walled Kitchen Garden where since 1999 the Henry Doubleday Research Association (now renamed Garden Organic), in conjunction with English Heritage, have been engaged on a re-creation of the vegetable and fruit garden of Victorian times. Originally established by the Countess of Portsmouth in 1753, it supplied the household requirements for most vegetables, fruit and flowers. That said, rather less is known about the supply of dairy produce, meat and malt for consumption by the household. The theme of this chapter is therefore to discuss some details of the Home Farm, its management and resources in the Victorian era and in particular to focus on the year 1851.

Estate Home Farms traditionally followed a conventional pattern of agriculture and with some notable exceptions were not centres of innovation and experiment. Their main function was to supply the needs of the household. While profit was not the main consideration the Home Farm was expected to pay its way and incur no loss and a profit if possible.

From the census taken on 30 March 1851, we learn that there were 39 people living at Audley End House, all of whom had to be catered for from the house kitchens. There may also have been staff who ate there but did not live in. The consumption of food was therefore considerable and the household was expected to be self supporting in food supplies. A high proportion of the farm output was sold to the 'Household'. Lesser amounts were sold to the other departments on the estate such as 'Coach & Riding Horse Stables', 'Game', 'Poultry' and so on. This is best illustrated by some approximate farm sales figures for 1851 which include 'Non Estate' sales (Table 1).[1]

Each year a valuation was carried out in January which listed and valued all the livestock and deadstock including crops in the ground described as 'in plant'.[2] The poultry were not included as they were part of a separate department. Some details of this 1851 valuation will be discussed next.

Table 1: Home Farm sales figures for 1851

Commodity	Sales to the Household & other named Estate Departments	Non-Estate Sales to various buyers
Value of livestock	75%	25%
Value of dairy produce	90%	10%
Barley including malt (vol)	60% poultry, game & dogs	40%
Wheat including flour (vol)	28% poultry, game & dogs	72%
Oats (vol)	48% mainly coach & saddle horse stables	Nil%

There were 18 farm horses and one filly foal. All of them had names, for example Boxer, Picture, Smiler, Sharper, Brag and so on. Apart from three, all were 'aged' and therefore over eight years old. Their total value was estimated at £353, ranging individually from £6 to

£33. They may have been of a nondescript type but some at least could have been Suffolk Punches, the clean-legged chestnut horses much favoured by East Anglian farmers, but today of concern to the Rare Breeds Survival Trust. Some of these horses were hired out to other departments on the estate such as the gardens and pleasure grounds for which they paid the farm. All survived until January 1852 except for one eight-year-old mare which was 'put down' during the year.

Fig. 2. Audley End House and east park, by William Tomkins 1788-9, showing the Shorthorn cattle kept there up to 1811 before they were sold and replaced by Alderneys.

The next group to consider are the cattle consisting firstly of 20 'milch cows', three in-calf heifers and nine yearling heifers. These dairy animals were in fact Jerseys but in 1851 still known as Alderneys. This dairy herd had been established at Audley End in July 1811, after a decision had been taken earlier that year to sell a herd of Yorkshire polled cattle (probably polled Shorthorns) and replace them with a specialised dairy breed, an unusual and innovative decision at that time (Fig. 2).[3] As these cattle at Audley End in 1851 were Jerseys, why were they known as Alderneys? Channel Island cattle had been imported into

England since the early 1700s destined normally for town dairies.[4] They were shipped to ports on the south coast usually Southampton. Records exist to show that for example between 1764 and 1775 there were 6,306 animals landed. Amongst these were French cattle which had to be imported via the Channel Islands to avoid excise duty. The last port of call for the cattle boats was Alderney before setting sail for England and it is thought that this was the reason that they were known in England as Alderneys and not Jerseys. Pedigree breeds as we know them today did not exist in the 18th century – they were simply types of cattle having certain characteristics. Selective breeding in the 19th century produced the pedigree animals most in demand that we would recognise today.

In the Home Farm accounts for 1811, the following entry records the payments made for Jersey cattle in July and September:

> Paid John Shurmer for 8 Alderney Cows and a bull £172 4s 0d
> Bill bringing cows from Southampton £8 15s 8d
> Gave Mr Shurmers man 2s 6d
> Wm Spicer's expenses to Southampton £4 8s 0d
>
> In September 1811:
>
> Paid Shurmer for 12 Cows, 3 Heifers, £257 10s 10d
> J. Nockolds Bill for Expenses on Journies £8 13s 6d
> Bill for bringing Cows from Southampton £12 3s 6d
> Paid Mollony for 1 Cow & 2 Heifers - Alderneys £42 7s 0d

These then were the foundation stock of the Audley End Jerseys which are recognised today as being the first pure-bred herd in England. John Shurmer was an importer of Jersey cattle, landing them at Southampton where the animals were offered for sale. From the records it would seem William Spicer was in charge of the first consignment and Jacob Nockolds, Audley End Land Steward, the second, as both incurred expenses on 'journies'. Before setting out for Audley End the animals would have been fitted with light iron plates to protect their feet. Travelling by the most direct route the journey would have been approximately 120 miles resulting in a droving cost as shown in the account. The route would have passed close to Billingbear, an estate in Berkshire owned by the Neville family where 'Mollony' was the Land Steward and from whom were purchased one Alderney cow and two heifers as shown in the account.

Home Farm herds existed to produce butter rather than fresh milk, or 'new milk' as it was described at the time and this was the situation at Audley End. The amount supplied is recorded and costed under the 'Housekeeping' heading in the monthly farm account. The dairymaid's wages were paid annually in December and from the census we learn she 'lived in'. Her work would have been conducted in the dairy, part of the Kitchen Court near the house.

Cattle from this herd were successfully shown at local agricultural shows in the 1830s and 1840s, and at the Essex County Show from 1858.[5] By the 1880s there were 18 Jersey herds within the county and of these, eight were within what we know today as Uttlesford District, several near Saffron Walden. Sadly the entire herd was sold at a dispersal sale at Audley End on 8 August 1902.[6] The remainder of the cattle in January 1851, apart from 14 calves, were 33 steers of various ages up to two years old amongst which were a group of 19 'Scotch Steers' probably purchased at one of the three Harlow Bush Fairs held each year on

Whit Monday, 9 September and 28 November. In October, 13 more Scotch Steers were paid for. Most of these animals were destined for the house kitchen but a few were sold to James Archer, a local butcher who also slaughtered cattle at Audley End.

The final livestock group to be considered were the sheep of which there were a total of 704 in January 1851, including 300 breeding ewes. They were Southdowns, the smallest of the compact close wool Downland breeds, at the time much in favour for their high quality carcases. In the 18th century the demand for large fatty joints of mutton and for tallow led to an emphasis on the horned breeds such as New Leicester. In the 1790s attention turned to the Southdown. After 1815 this breed and other Downland breeds were developed to take advantage of the new arable systems with the intensive cultivation of arable fodder crops to satisfy the demand for good quality mutton – the conversion of turnips into mutton.

They are recorded at Audley End in 1811 valued at £2 each for the 399 breeding ewes. Interestingly, also recorded were seven Merino ewes valued at £14 5s 0d each. The Southdown breed had been greatly improved by John Ellman of Glynde in Sussex, who had taken over his father's farm in 1780. His work was much admired by the Duke of Bedford, Coke of Norfolk and other leading farmers. He died in 1852. Locally Jonas Webb of Babraham was the noted Southdown flockmaster and his memorial statue is to be seen today in the centre of Babraham. He died in 1862. Over the years there were livestock transactions between Audley End Farm and Babraham.

Arthur Young, writing in 1807, about Audley End Farm said that 'they were getting into Southdown having previously had the Norfolk breed' and 'that Southdowns were spreading everywhere in Essex'.[7] Following a conversation with Mr Nockolds he learnt that the extensive lawns at Audley End must be kept close fed for beauty: and could be considered only as sheep walks'. A very environmentally-friendly way of lawn maintenance of which the present-day Garden Organic (formerly the Henry Doubleday Research Association) would doubtless approve!

This flock was sold at the dispersal sale mentioned above on 8 August 1902. That concludes the review of the livestock in 1851. The deadstock was also subject to an annual valuation in January which consisted of the estimated quantities of farm produce in store resulting from the harvest of the previous year, 1850, and which reveals the many different crops grown (Table 2).

Table 2: Quantities of farm produce, 1850

Crops	Quantity in store	Total
Wheat	260 quarters	58½ tons
Barley	230 quarters	46 tons
Oats	360 quarters	54 tons
Malt	7 quarters	-
Potatoes	250 bushels	6¼ tons
Carrots	1000 bushels	25 tons
Mangel Wurzels		100 tons
Hay (various sorts)		208 tons
Wool	86 tods	1 ton approx.

Note: The quarter is a measure of volume containing eight bushels. The bushel weight varies from one commodity to another. Wool is weighed in tods: one tod = 28 lb.

The acreage of crops 'autumn sown' and turnips still in the ground from the previous year are described as 'in plant'. These were shown as follows: wheat 60 acres, rye 14 acres, clover 83 acres and turnips 65 acres, making a total of 222 acres. It is probable that the farm was some 400 acres in extent and the 18 working horses kept would agree with this figure. The final part of the Deadstock Valuation is concerned with farm equipment valued at £440. It consisted of 11 wagons, 12 carts, ploughs, harrows, other implements and finally 'horse gears' or harnesses.

Having looked in some detail at the resources of the farm, what of the men who worked here and whose monthly wages are recorded in the farm accounts? There were three senior skilled men employed, each responsible for their group of livestock and normally assisted by less experienced workers, some of them juveniles. Firstly, John Gipp the carter, who would have been a very important person on the farm. He had the responsibility for ensuring fit horses ready for a day's work and the general management of the farm stable, also the make-up of the horse teams for field work and road haulage would all be his responsibility.

Joseph Webb was the shepherd who would have had overall control of all the sheep and the successful lambing of the 300 Southdown ewes. He had been recommended for the Shepherd's Prize back in 1840. His two sons worked with him. The third skilled worker was the cowman and responsible for the dairy herd and their milking performance, calf rearing and day-to-day herd management. The latter two workers lived in Audley End village.

These then were senior livestock men, but there was one other, the yardsman, whose pay was twice that of any other employee. He was Thomas Simmons, probably the foreman and responsible for the general day-to-day work on the farm including allocating labour to the various jobs in hand. According to the 1851 census he lived at the Home Farm, then known as Duck Street Farm, as did John Gipp the carter close to his horses.

Another five men spent most of their year ploughing, thus employing ten of the 18 horses kept. Then, there were five, sometimes six men 'jobbing', mainly the same people each month. One can only speculate on their work, but probably it included hedging, ditching, hoeing and general farm work. In addition to those adults, there were normally eight boys, judging by their pay, who worked alongside the yardsman, carter, shepherd, and cowman. Finally there were many named workers who appeared to be employed on 'piece work' carrying out all manner of jobs, for example grinding turnips, collecting twitch, sorting potatoes, filling dung carts, spreading and knocking dung, attending to threshing machine and so on and so forth. Extra money was earned at harvest time and paid out in addition to the men's regular wages in September, followed by the harvest supper. Many of these men lived in Audley End village. It is apparent from the farm accounts, there were opportunities for weekend work with the livestock, allowances for drilling corn, payments for catching rats and sparrows and for 'attending to horses' often at weekends and several other part-time activities.

In the December 1851 account an item is included: 'other profits'. This records the sales of hides, skins and 2,159 lb of fat at 3d per pound to James Archer, the butcher. This would represent the sales over a twelve-month period. Also charged for is farriery (shoeing) for horses used in garden and pleasure grounds, plus a proportion of the wheelwright's and collar-maker's bills. Wood for the fires in the house also had to be paid for as was 'Keepers Horses at Grass 93 days or 13 weeks 2 days at 3s, £1 19s 10d'. This was followed by other maintenance costs related to the 'keepers horses'. Finally, the following: 'Labour of horses to sundry fields that are in hand on the Estate' - but not part of Home Farm. Little or nothing which could enhance the farm profit escaped the eagle eye of the Land Steward.

At the end of the year, a 'Summary of Farm Accounts for 1851' was drawn up showing payments and receipts for each month. The receipts were £3,472 3s 7½d and the payments were £2,870 13s 1d, leaving a favourable balance of £601 10s 6½d. Deducted from this was a 'Decrease in the value of the Stock £98 13s leaving a final profit of £502 17s 6½d. This was accounted for in the following manner: 'Rental made of the Farm £502 17s 6½d'.

This farm may not have been exceptionally innovative in the way it was managed, but it had moved with the times during a period of considerable change and was very well run by competent agriculturalists who maintained meticulous farm records. The Jersey herd and the Southdown flock were amongst the most progressive in the country and justly renowned for being high quality livestock.

3
Horham Hall Farm, Thaxted 1807

About one and a half miles out of Thaxted on the Broxted- Elsenham road (B1051) near Armigers Farm, there is a private road leading to Horham Hall, which is shown on the map (Fig. 3). In 1807, the Hall was the centre of an estate of some 900 acres containing six farms, a water mill and some woodland, all located in the parishes of Thaxted and Broxted (Fig. 4). The estate had passed in 1617 into the possession of Sir William Smyth, nephew and heir of the Learned Sir Thomas Smyth, Secretary of State, who had built Hill Hall (now English Heritage) at Theydon Garnon, Essex. The estate remained in the ownership of this family until 1854 but some 320 acres were offered for sale by auction in July 1824.[1]

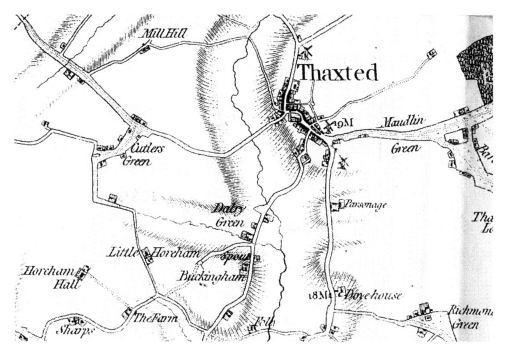

Fig. 3. Extract from Chapman & André map of Essex 1777, showing Thaxted and Horham Hall. The parish boundary between Thaxted and Broxted parishes runs through the hall.

The farm at Horham Hall was the subject of an inventory and valuation on 14-15 September 1807 undertaken by John Barnard, a valuer based at Tilty, the small parish adjoining Thaxted and Broxted. Mary Buttle – sometimes spelt with only one 't' – the farm tenant had recently died and had been buried at Broxted on 26 August 1807.[2] She left a will dated 2 March 1802 which had been proved on 8 September 1807.[3] The record of the actual inventory and valuation is in itself of local historical interest because it is contained in one of the 45 notebooks covering the day-to-day work of John Barnard, Valuer and Appraiser between 1782 and 1786 and from 1803 to 1825.[4] The 40 or 50 notebooks in the collection examined so far are all of a similar size and type, approximately 8x5 inches, leather-bound and secured by a small brass clip. They are written-up using ink. The valuations on each page are totalled up and that figure is transferred to a summary page at the end of any particular set of work to produce a grand total. However, whilst Barnard used explicit £.s.d. symbols for the totals of each group such as cattle, granary, cart lodge etc., for the individual items he used a lettered code thus keeping these values to himself. The exceptions to this practice were the valuations of crops and the value of field cultivations recently carried out. For these he again used £.s.d.

Apart from complete farms there are valuations of grass crops, crops in the ground, tillages and many other aspects of farming. In addition, private houses, shops, workshops, tools and stocks in trade were all subject to valuation at various times. The majority are concerned with the effects of deceased persons. Unfortunately this part of the collection does not include any auctioneers' notebooks for this early 'John Barnard period' but there are some from 1815 onwards which do show the actual prices achieved at auction with buyers' names and the expenses Barnard charged. By 1809 Robert Franklin had joined the business, probably as an assistant and later as a partner, and became the sole owner by 1825.

Fig. 4. Horham Hall, Thaxted, drawn by J. Greig for Excursions through Essex (1819).

The Buttles

In order to put this farm valuation in context some background information on Mary Buttle's family will be helpful. Her father, Robert died in 1763 and left everything to his widow Susanna.[5] He described himself as a farmer of Broxted. Susanna Buttle died in 1774 and she left her wearing apparel and linen to be equally divided between her four daughters, including Mary. To her three sons, and the above mentioned four daughters, she left her securities, cattle, corn, farming stock, household goods, other chattels and personal estate to be equally divided, 'part and share alike'. There are one or two other provisions which exclude one further son and one further daughter 'already provided for'.[6] This then was a family with substantial assets, as will be confirmed by the 1807 valuation of 'the effects of Mary Buttle'. It would seem that during the intervening years from 1774 to the year of her death in 1807, she had become the sole owner of all the tenant stock at Horham Hall Farm. Apart from two cash bequests, one to her brother Robert (who farmed at Dairy Green Farm, Thaxted, then part of the estate), and one to her sister Jane, she left everything else to her sister Ann and her nephew and niece Robert and Millicent. Her sister Jane was married to John Salmon at Folly Mill, Monk Street, Thaxted.[7]

Cheese-making

On reading this 1807 valuation I was struck by two points. Firstly, amongst all those already looked at, here was the first one which was concerned with a woman farmer, surely an unusual occurrence at the time. There is no reason why she should not have farmed extremely well, but still it was unusual. However, an explanation was at hand with a clue when I noted that there was a herd of no less than 18 cows. Eighteen cows can produce a great deal of milk, so what was their purpose? This became clear in the second half of the valuation concerned with the 'household' and the contents of the various rooms. After the kitchen valuation all was revealed in 'The Cheese Room' where there were 238 cheeses of two types and three ages valued at £97 18s 1d and, I estimate, weighing just over two tons. The dairy and cheese room have always been the preserves of women, highly skilled in the careful production of fine cheese and butter. The success of English cheese-making throughout the ages has depended on the work of women. By 1807 farmhouse cheese-making in Essex had become something of a rarity, although a little was still produced. Charles Vancouver, writing in 1795 said:

> This neighbourhood [Steeple Bumpstead] was very famous formerly for the manufacturing of cheese, but of late years the dairy business has generally given place to the suckling of calves for the London market... it may have been that the demand for veal in the London markets of late years has rendered suckling more profitable than the cheese dairy; or that the farmers' wives and daughters of Steeple Bumpstead are no longer the notable painstaking laborious race which established the fame of the North Essex cheeses... cheese can now be made and conveyed to market by water-carriage with full profit from a distance too great for the production of veal for the London market.[8]

Veal was conveyed in wicker baskets wrapped in damp cloths so it required rapid delivery. There are some further interesting references to Essex cheese at Hempstead. Arthur Young wrote in 1807:

> Dairy cattle at Hempstead are Long Horned Derby. He makes two meal cheese. That is the night milk is skimmed and mixed with the morning fresh. He sells at 7d to 8d per lb but 6d a more general price. I ate some of his cheese at Mr Ruggles' [Finchingfield] table and found it

excellent. A wey [256 lb] per cow reckoned a common produce. They are bought in at three years old at £13 to £17 per cow and are attentive not to keep them so long as to lessen much their value as fatting stock. The Derbys when turned out from the dairy or sold, fatten well, better they think than Suffolks.[9]

He then goes on to talk about the 'Hay cheese' – that produced in winter:

Not much straw is eaten after Christmas when they have hay given of which a cow will eat two loads if permitted. They have no turnips as the country is too heavy …in summer they consume the produce [grass] of two acres each.

There is a further observation on the grassland:

The best of our pastures are to be found in parishes and neighbourhoods of Epping, Harlow, Broxstead, Dunmow and Bumpstead. Our meadows are chiefly on the banks of our several rivers Lea, Roding, Chelmer, Colne which do abundantly water and fertilize our meadows.

Arthur Young gives some annual costings for dairy farming around 1807. On the income side he shows sales of cheese at £6 10s, £4 4s for butter, £2 for a calf and £1 for pigs fed on the dairy by-products, one supposes. The total is £13 14s. The cost per cow per year without apparently including their capital cost amount is £11 18s, leaving a margin of only £1 16s per cow per annum. There would of course be the eventual sale of the fat cow when her milking days were over. However, it is no surprise that farmhouse cheese production was in the doldrums in Essex!

Fig. 5. Unloading cheese from a carrier's broad-wheeled wagon into a cheese-monger's cart. Drawn by W. H. Pyne who travelled widely at the end of the 18th century.

The cheese room at Horham Hall Farm in 1807 contained the stock of cheeses shown below:

13 Old cheeses valued at £7 3s 0d (6½ lb)
19 Hay cheeses valued at £5 8s 0d (4½ lb)
207 Two Meal cheeses valued at £85 17s 1d (5d lb)

Thirteen old cheeses, fully matured, were the most valuable at 6½d per lb – Arthur Young quoted 6d, 7d or 8d per lb – with the new as yet unmatured, 'Two Meal Cheeses' made during the summer of 1807 valued at 5d per lb. Lastly, the less highly regarded 'Hay Cheeses' – winter made cheese – at 4½d per lb. These individual cheeses appeared to be 20 lb each in weight with rather less for the 'Hay Cheeses'.

The dairy cows calved in the spring each year and produced their highest yields of milk from the protein-rich summer grass. In the winter they would be kept in yards with some partial covering and were fed mainly on hay, hence the title 'Hay Cheese'. However, the secondary purpose for yarding stock in the winter was to produce the farmyard manure essential for maintaining land fertility. Distribution to the retailers of cheese was undertaken by cheesemongers who acted as middlemen between producer and retailer. They were not always popular with producers. Transport of the cheese to urban centres would be handled by land carriers as shown in the illustration (Fig. 5).

Other crops

Horham Hall Farm was not only concerned with cheese-making, as the valuation in 1807 shows. Harvest would have been nearing completion by the date of the valuation on 14 and 15 September. There were 43 acres of wheat, mostly Rivet, a bearded red-grained variety valued at £405. Barley amounted to 37 acres, valued at £214. Oats and peas, oats, peas, beans and tares amounted to a further 31 acres valued at £142. There were two acres of peas but in the opinion of the valuer 'not worth the expense of cutting and harvesting'. The total harvest was valued at £761. In addition there were 40 loads of hay valued at £120 cut from about 35 acres, I estimate. The valuation then continues with the 'Tillages' which were the summer cultivations of fallow land being prepared for the following year's crops. The only way, at that time, to keep heavy land free from weeds was to fallow it, probably every third year. There were 58 acres under fallow in 1807. The cost of all the cultivations was assessed and, together with the value of the farmyard manure applied, were valued in total at £91 15s 2d. Amongst these cultivations was the use of a Shym or Shim, sometimes twice on the same field. The purpose of this implement was to cut through the weed growth below the surface of the ground. To do this a flat blade was drawn through the soil which needed to be ridged up before. Arthur Young writing in 1807 described this operation in the following way:

> Mr Hale at Bulmer [Essex] uses a ridge Shim which I saw at work and it performed perfectly well. He had summer-fallowed on 2 bout ridges on which the thistles and other weeds had got up: the cutting blade of the Shim carried a ridge at a time, and cut to its base, leaving all weeds to die and the ridge only a little flattened: a stout lad and a pair of horses worked it. The beam close to the block is occasionally loaded by twisting a heavy chain around it. Mr Ruggles of Spain Hall has one on which the boy rides if necessary.[10]

I understand that Mr Ruggles was the inventor of this implement.

The Stock

The final part of the farm valuation is concerned with the remaining livestock and deadstock. Eight farm horses were kept valued at between £11 and £40 each. There was also a pony valued at £8 and 22 pigs and some ewes and lambs. All these livestock were valued by using the lettered code referred to earlier.

The deadstock was scattered around various buildings in the farmyard. The Cart Lodge contained two harvest wagons, three carts, one tumbril (tipcart) and one road wagon. Road wagons were normally kept by the larger farmers who not only transported their own produce to market and canal-head but also sought out 'land carriage' work and backloads to keep the wheels turning and money coming in. The farm implements - four ploughs and some harrows - seems to be somewhat minimal for a large farm. There is no mention of the shim discussed above, nor was there any roller or ridger.

The farming stock and crops in total were valued at £1575 3s 5d. The contents of the farmhouse, with which we are not concerned in detail, amounted to a further £245 4s 6d, making a total valuation of the tenant's assets of £1820 7s 11d. There is no mention in this valuation of any further assets such as cash in the house, cash in the bank, money out on loan, nor of any securities held by Mary Buttle. It should therefore not be regarded as a statement of her total wealth but as a farm valuation which would affect the incoming farm tenant taking over the farm assets. The acreage of the farm seems to have been some 280-300 acres. A survey of the estate conducted in 1749 shows Horham Hall being 314 acres but there may well have been some rearrangement of estate land by 1807.[11]

This concludes an analysis of Horham Hall Farm in the early 19th century. There is much that can be learnt about the way farms were run by examining similar valuations together with reading contemporary writings. Little seems to be known about cheese-making in North Essex, so I hope this contribution will throw some light on a long-lost craft. On a lighter note, in *The English Countryman*, G.E. Fussell quotes John Hayward:

> I never saw a Banbury cheese thick enough
> But I have seen Essex cheese quick enough!

4

Mitchells Farm at Little Walden: its life and times

Fig. 6. Mitchells Farm near Little Walden.

To have any information on the history of one farm from soon after the Norman Conquest to the present day is indeed a rare occurrence. Mitchells has always been a freehold property occupied by tenants until 1967 (Fig. 6). Historically it lay within part of the manor of Chipping Walden.

The story begins sometime after the Norman Conquest when Mitchells probably originated in the same way as the adjoining farm named Cloptons, first mentioned in 1303 as a peasant freeholding.[1] We do not have any record of the original size but it is likely that the land would have been cleared from an original assart (private farmland formed out of common land) of the native woodland to form a compact farm of several small arable fields and pastures. A tenant, or husbandman would have been in occupation. There is some evidence that during this early period Mitchells was part of the manor of Bendish Hall at Radwinter in the Deanery of Sampforde and later, as we shall see, was owned by the Convent of St Saviours, Faversham Abbey in Kent. Members of the Cornell family are mentioned as tenants and by 1521 William Cornell, 'husbandman', was in occupation of both Mitchells Farm and Bendish Hall.[2]

Most of the Mitchells land is on or about the 100 metre contour which in North-west Essex is likely to mean that the soil will be heavy chalky boulder clay, slowly permeable but well-structured, overlying a sub-soil with impeded drainage. This soil type was derived from chalky glacial drift deposited during the Ice Age. The lighter soils in the immediate area are closely associated with the river valleys but they are not generally found on this farm. Until field drainage was installed in the 18th and 19th centuries, cereal crop yields of about 4½ hundredweight per acre would be adversely affected by conditions of impeded drainage (water-logging) especially in very wet winters. A medieval farmer ploughing with four or maybe six oxen drawing the heavy English plough needed to penetrate heavy land, would find this difficult work for much of the year. Plough horses began to replace oxen from the 13th century onwards but only slowly. Horses were expensive to keep and old oxen could be fattened for the market.

Mitchells Farm is situated at the junction in North-west Essex between what Oliver Rackham describes as 'The Ancient Countryside' and 'The Planned Countryside'.[3] To the north and west there were vast areas of common open-fields farmed in strips, but in the 18th and 19th centuries subject to enclosure awards. This type of country was known as 'champion' and was closely associated with Cambridgeshire and the south Midlands. To the south of Mitchells and including most of Little Walden and Ashdon the country changes quite markedly. Here we find predominately early enclosed lands creating individual isolated small farms, each having its own hedged fields, connected by footpaths and meandering roads and tracks. Small woods and ponds are common with oak and ash trees predominating. This pattern of settlement was known as 'severalty'. The difference between the two types of countryside, even to this day, is quite evident, although enclosure of the 'champion' country destroyed the open-field strip patterns. To the south-west of Mitchells there was one common open field named North Field which in 1605 had 21 tenants farming there, the largest with six enclosed acres and the smallest with half a rood, the majority with 1 to 1½ acres each. One tenant had nine strips, the Lord six, and the rest anything from five to one: an administrative headache for the farmers and the manor stewards.

The 16th and 17th centuries

In July 1538 Sir Richard Riche was granted the ownership of the manor of Bendish Hall, Mitchells Farm and other tenements and fields in this part of Essex, the Convent of St Saviours, Faversham having been dissolved.[4] Thus it was that Mitchells passed into secular hands after a long period of ownership by the church. From the *History of Sir Richard Riche* (1496-1567) we learn that:

> Few were more rapacious or had better opportunities for profiting by the dissolution of the monasteries: the manors he secured in Essex alone covered a considerable portion of the county. It should, however, be acknowledged that he used some of his ill-gotten wealth for a noble object... In 1554 he founded a chaplaincy at Felsted and in May 1564 Riche founded a grammar school at Felsted which afforded education to two sons of Oliver Cromwell.

His ownership was comparatively brief because by 1554 Mitchells had passed into the hands of a long-established family at Linton named Parris or Parish. They were Royalist gentry whose lands were seized by the Parliamentary side during the Civil War because of their Popish recusancy, but were recovered in 1658. They also owned land at Pudding Norton in Norfolk but by 1675 they had sold Mitchells to Sir Thomas Sclaters, another Royalist who owned Ashdon Hall. Upon his death in 1736 Mitchells and some other properties were left to his 'Kinswoman', Sarah King. More of this family later.[5]

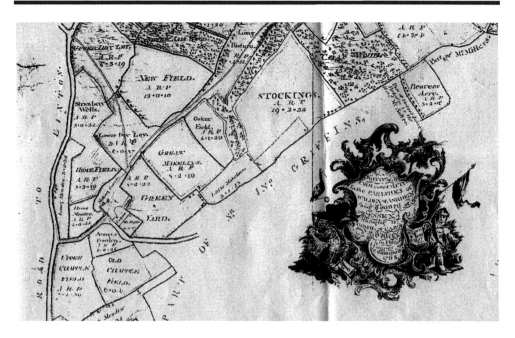

Fig. 7. Mitchells Farm, extract from map of 1768 showing the farm in both Saffron Walden and Ashdon. It was surveyed and drawn by Joseph Freeman, Cambridge.

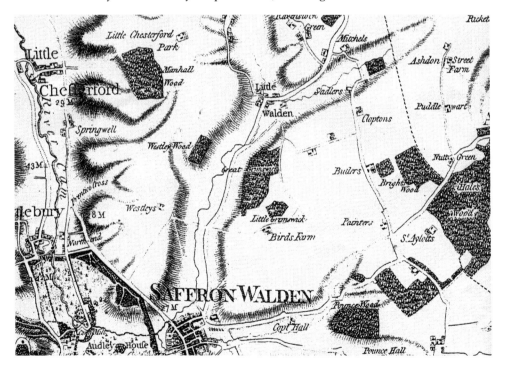

Fig. 8. Chapman & André map of 1777 showing Mitchells north-east of Little Walden.

A translated copy of The Field Book of Walden, although written up in 1758 for John Griffen Griffen Esq, the future 1st Lord Braybrooke, records details of all the manorial lands held within Chipping Walden as they were in 1605. That part of Mitchells situated in Ashdon parish is not therefore included.[6] About Mitchells the following is recorded:

> The Tenement Mitchells. Mr Parish (*sic*) the Farm called Michells (*sic*) late H. Bretton with divers enclosed grounds both free and copy appertenment containing by estimation about 140 Acres in all: where of 38 Acres 3 Roods are noted to be holden by copy and rent of 21/8d charged upon...[7]

Mr Parrish also held a further 11 acres called Great Ashwells which lay at a distance of about one mile south-west from the Mitchells homestead. From the will of Charles Parris, owner of Mitchells who died in 1658, we know that the farm buildings then in existence were two barns, one stable, one cowhouse and the farmhouse itself.[8] These early farm buildings were probably replaced by more modern structures in the 18th century and the farmhouse was probably modernised and maybe enlarged at that time.

The 18th century

The earliest record we have is an extract of the Ashdon Parish Tithe Account for 1730 showing details of the Mitchells farmland situated in Ashdon parish. It shows the tenant was Thomas Robinson who occupied 91 acres 3 roods 21 perches divided into nine fields. Of these, six were in fallow totalling 39 acres, 35 acres were growing winter cereals (Forecrop) and 16 acres were into spring sown crops (Earthcrop). While no tithe was payable on the fallow ground, it was payable on the remainder amounting to £8 16s 11d. The high percentage of fallow (43%) may be misleading, the explanation being that this 39 acres was part of a total farm of 242 acres. The Saffron Walden part of the farm probably had, in that year, proportionately less fallow. One would expect to find roughly a third of the total arable acreage in fallow in any one year.

We have no farm accounts for Mitchells for these or any later years to show what the farm was producing. This is not unusual. However, for an adjoining farm named Little Walden Park we do have their farm accounts for 1747-49 which record in detail the income and payments made.[9] It is likely Mitchells was farmed in a similar manner so these accounts are relevant. Little Walden Park was 'in hand' (farmed by the owner) from 1745-48 for want of a tenant. A new tenancy lease was taken up by John Fuller on 29 September 1748. The farm belonged to the Audley End Estate and at the time was very run down and much money was being spent on it to get it into good order to attract a suitable tenant.[10] Total acreage was 358 divided into 200 acres arable, 135 pasture and 23 woodland, so somewhat larger than Mitchells. For the period January 1747 to November 1748 the account shows the farm sales totalling £649, of which 37% was derived from livestock, 55% from cereals and 8% from miscellaneous sales. Sales of 121 sheep of various types were the most important livestock contributor followed by 13 fat cattle and 36 various pigs, mainly fat hogs. Total livestock sales amounted to £241. Of the cereals, barley was the principle earner with 40 tons sold, followed by 26 tons of oats but only 12½ tons of wheat. Total cereal sales were £354. The account clearly illustrates the importance attached to livestock sales at that time and, secondly, the high volume of barley and oat sales. However the average price per quarter (8 bushels) of wheat, barley and oats were respectively 29s, 15s 5d and 12s. The limitation on growing more wheat was that it needed to be grown on clean ground following a fallow year.

Not unexpectedly the farm made a profit but no rent had been paid, nor was interest on 'tenants' capital' taken into account. The rent for the new tenant taking over in 1748 for a nine-year lease was £200 per annum, which would exclude any rent for woodland, no doubt retained 'in hand' by the estate. This works out at about 12s per acre for the arable and pasture.

There is one other interesting item shown in the account for May 1747: six tons of turnips had been paid for, bought from Thomas Pennystone Junior for £6. His father was the Land Steward (previously mentioned) of Audley End Estate. These turnips were for 'fatting wether sheep' (no doubt over-wintered lambs - 'hoggetts').Thomas Pennystone Junior was the tenant at North End Farm situated in the Cam valley. He would have been well placed to grow and lift turnips during the previous winter on the light valley land he farmed, whereas this would not have been possible on the Little Walden Park Farm chalky boulder clay.

The same limitation would apply to Mitchells. Growing turnips for livestock revolutionised the east of England farming practices, as it made possible the discontinuation of the wasteful 'fallow break'. Turnips grown in rows were regarded as a cleaning crop, as well as providing winter feed for livestock. To grow well, and to lift in the winter, required lightish land.

In 1758 the then owner of Mitchells, Mrs Martha King, sold the farm to Gonville & Caius College, Cambridge. The following is an extract from the Chronicle of the College Estates which sets out the details of the sale:

> 250 acres, 2 roods of Farm and 42 acres of Wood was bought of Mrs M. King for Mr Wortleys Benefaction - price £4136 10s and £74 10s 6d was spent on Manor Fines and Fees. It is in the parishes of Little Walden and Ashdon. The Messuage with 34 acres 1 rood of arable and pasture and 10 acres of woodland were copyhold of the manor of Chipping Walden.

The earliest farm map we have of Mitchells is dated 1768 (Fig. 7). This shows the complete farm in both Walden and Ashdon parishes. It was surveyed and drawn for Gonville & Caius College by Joseph Freeman. No doubt as a result of further clearances the farm had grown to 273 acres and there was a further 60 acres of woodland 'in hand' (see also Fig. 8, map of 1777).

Before leaving the 18th century there is one further relevant record to look at. This is another tithe record for Ashdon contained in a notebook which belonged to the Revd J. North and covers the period 1792 to1810.[11] Up to 1792 the titheable area of land in Ashdon parish was 102 acres. In a calculation in 1792 the acreage was increased to 125 acres and the payment due was now to be £18 18s 0d per annum or 3s 9d per acre for nine years from Michaelmas 1792. The tithe payment due in 1730 had been £8 16s 11d. Although changes were made to tithe dues over the years, payments were only finally extinguished by the Tithe Act 1936. Collection of unredeemed tithe dues was only abandoned in 1977.

From about 1792 and on into the first part of the 19th century, members of the Adams family were the tenants. John Player, writing in his *Sketches of Saffron Walden* dated 1845, recalls:

Adams of Mitchells (not the old Adams - he had been dead long before) was a patronymic for many years so truly familiar to every parochial mind, that we miss the good man on juries, in the market, and on the road; and while we imperceptibly sigh after fallen fellows, while we think of his blue coat and gilt buttons as something of a Windsor uniform – the distinguished attire peculiar at that period to the Lord of Mitchells.

The 19th century

The century started off in buoyant mood for farmers and landowners. The threat of blockade and invasion by the French helped to push up farm produce prices followed by increased land values and rents. Peace came in 1815 and with it the rapid discharge of men from the Army and Navy and this produced low wages and distress, and a great surplus of rural labourers without work. During the war years farmers had learnt to farm without any excess labour, having adopted more advanced practices. There was a general reduction in grain prices from 1815 to 1837. The Corn Laws, which had protected British agriculture, were repealed in 1846 and a free market in grain was established. For many years the effect was minimal but by the third quarter of the century grain and later livestock products from the 'New World', impacted on prices in the home market. The predominantly grain producers of the eastern counties, and Essex in particular, were unable to compete and to farm profitably. Added to which there was a series of bad harvests around 1879 which added to their problems.

Locally over the immediate post-war period there was a succession of bad harvests causing wheat prices to rise and making relief necessary. Then in 1813 there was a severe frost commencing on 26 December which lasted with little respite until 20 March 1814. At Mitchells the Adams family continued as tenants probably up to about 1840 when the tenancy changed hands and George Bolton occupied the farm. Between 1868 and 1871 further woodland was cleared to increase the useable farm acreage. Then in 1869 the off-lying land at Great Ashwells, approximately one mile south-west of Mitchells, was exchanged for land nearer home with the Gibson family of Saffron Walden. They were established farmers in Little Walden. In 1872 a block of four red-brick cottages were built, which still stand today along the Hadstock-Walden road near Mitchells.

As the century progressed so Mitchells would have become less of a mixed farm and a more specialised arable unit deriving most of its income from wheat and barley. By mid-century Essex had become a county with approximately 75% of its farmland in arable crops.[12] Grassland only remained significant on land, in the main, unsuitable for cropping. In only seven parishes out of 300 did pasture exceed arable. During this period Mitchells would probably have kept in yards bought-in cattle purchased in the autumn and sold fat the following spring. There was a dual purpose in this practice. Firstly, to profit from cattle fed largely on arable by-products and oilseed cake, but secondly to produce the farmyard manure so essential to maintaining soil fertility. Little or no grassland, except some for hay, was necessary with this system and the yards would be cleared when the cattle were sold.

Of all the advances to improve crop yields in Essex, the most significant, especially on the heavy boulder clay found on Mitchells, was the continuing work of under-drainage. Farmers were well aware of the fact that impeded drainage led to water-logging of the rooting zone of crops and resulted in poor and shallow root development. As there was a summer soil moisture deficit in most years, crop yields were thus limited.

In the 18th century, as early as 1727, Essex had led the way in field drainage. Hand-dug deep field drains at intervals of 12 yards apart were connected to a main drain leading into a ditch. Prior to the invention of drainage tiles (pipes of various shapes and sizes) around 1840, the bottom of the drainage trench was covered with compacted brushwood cut from nearby hedges. Above this a layer of compacted straw was placed before the trench was refilled with soil. This apparently primitive method of under draining was acknowledged to be very successful and lasted 15-20 years and would certainly cover the period of any long lease. It became known as 'The Essex Method'. Tenants were expected to do the work but landlords may have provided some assistance. The high labour requirement for trench digging was the main expense and cost at the time from £4 to £8 per acre. This work would have probably been carried out at Mitchells, but during the 19th century more advanced replacement systems would have been installed.

According to the *Record of Secular Monuments* (1913), Mitchells farmhouse was built in the early 17th century with a later small extension at the rear. The construction was of timber frame and plaster with some brick, under a slated roof. It appears to be of a 'Lobby Entrance' type (a modern classification) with alterations and small additions mainly of 19th century origin.[13] The existing timber barn is likely to date from the early 18th century, as a beam is stamped with the initials 'TW' and a date 1713. The 'TW' refers to Thomas Webb whose family and forebears had connections with Ashdon parish. Another beam is stamped '27 October 1851 RB & JA', probably relating to some repairs carried out at that time. The Bolton family were tenants in 1841 and 1851. Beyond the barn is an extensive first-floor granary addition.

The 20th century

In 1910 Gonville & Caius College sold Mitchells farm to Sir James Lyle Mackay, later Lord Inchcape, who at the time owned the Chesterford Park Estate. It remained part of the estate until 1916 when the whole estate of some 3250 acres was offered for sale by auction at the Town Hall, Saffron Walden on 3 October. Lot 8 was Mitchells farm extending to 301.133 acres with a rental value of £257 10s per annum, and included a 'nicely situated farm house, a row of four cottages, excellent buildings, good arable and grass land and several well-grown woods'. The sale notice then goes on to list the farm buildings as follows:

> Nine loose boxes, five-bay open cattle shed, barn, mixing house, three-bay open cattle shed, stable for eight, chaff house, granary, three-bay open cattle shed, two workshops and coal shed, five-bay open cart shed, trap house, two-stall nag stable, and loose box, tool house, two open implement sheds, two loose boxes and three piggeries.

In addition to all the above were another set of buildings known as Littleys, consisting of an 'eight-bay open shed, five-bay open shed, barn, stable for two ranged round a cattle yard'. Before passing into the hands of S.J. Burgess in 1933 the estate passed into various ownerships with which we need not concern ourselves. In 1937 the estate was bought by Dr Werner Gothe and was not sold again until 1961 when it was purchased by The Duke Trust. In 1967, for the first time in the long history of Mitchells, it was purchased by the occupier and tenant, Mr William Gordon Tinney. His brother Arthur Tinney, farmer, pig-breeder and market gardener, had become the tenant in 1923 and his younger brother William Gordon took over in 1936. Today Mitchells is farmed by his son Mr Roger Tinney, whose late wife Coral compiled the notes on which this chapter is based.

In 1942 work started on Little Walden Airfield in preparation for occupation by the USAAF. The legacy of this extensive wartime airfield is still to be seen today by the presence of concrete roadways, control tower and hangar. Little Walden Park was the principle area affected, but some land on Mitchells and the adjacent Monks Hall farm was also used. It was not until 1958 that all the land was returned to agriculture and reclamation commenced.

The history of this one farm in North-west Essex, described in brief in this chapter, is typical of many others where over the centuries men and women have toiled to produce good food for the nation. Hopefully they will be able to continue to do so in spite of current difficulties.

5

The floor malting industry of North-west Essex and East Hertfordshire up to *c.*1914

In some parts of England growing barley for malting took precedence over growing wheat for milling. North-west Essex and East Hertfordshire has been one such area. During the late 20th century the importance attached to the wheat crop increased and malting barley has become almost the Cinderella of cereal growing except on the lightest land. The purpose of this chapter is to place the local malting industry of Saffron Walden in its regional setting and to demonstrate how it functioned over its long history. Much has already been written, of a mainly technical and economic nature, about the subject of malting, so a range of literature has been consulted to compile this chapter. Special acknowledgement must be made to two important works which, in chronological terms, cover the period from 1700-1914: *The Brewing Industry in England 1700-1830* by Peter Mathias of Downing College, Cambridge; and *The British Malting Industry since 1830* by Christine Clark.

Saffron Walden from the mid-18th to the early-19th century was the greatest malting centre in Essex, but its importance after that declined and it ceased to produce any malt around 1960 (Fig. 9). Other centres in the region continued to operate but even Ware, the region's malting capital, finally ceased production in 1994.

Part One

The background and regional setting

Before the Industrial Revolution, industry was concerned largely with the processing of the products of agriculture. Locally, at various times in history, wool, saffron, corn and livestock have all been important products which had to be processed and marketed. Corn can be conveniently divided into wheat for milling, subsequently made into bread and barley for malting to be used in brewing beer and ale, the common beverages for all the people before the days of tea drinking in the 19th century. Originally ale was an unhopped sweet malt liquor as distinct from beer. Nationally more barley was grown than wheat because it will tolerate a wider range of soil and climatic conditions. In times of wheat shortage, possibly following a poor harvest, some barley was used to make barley bread as a substitute for the more desirable and more expensive wheaten bread. Somewhere between 65% and 70% of the national barley crop was normally converted into malt for the brewers. Arthur Young writing in 1808 confirmed this figure.[1]

Some of this early malt would have been of indifferent quality if judged by later more exacting standards. Gregory King, the 17th century statistician, thought the average family spent more each week on beer than on any other single item. Farm labourers' wages were supplemented by beer allowances and William Marshall, chairman of the Board of Agriculture, writing in 1790 complained about the waste of malt and gave examples of some beer and ale allowances: 'In hay and corn harvest the customary allowance is a gallon of beer a man (in hot weather they drink more) and besides this mowers expect 2 quarts of ale and never less than one. With some difficulty I got turnip hoers to accept two quarts of beer and one of ale: they wanted two of beer and two of ale.'[2]

Fig. 9. Barnards Malting, High Street, Saffron Walden.

Much of this beer would have been brewed on the farm from local supplies of malt. Very many farm and cottage inventories recorded by F. W. Steer include references to malt, malt houses, and kell houses (kiln houses).[3] These were quite small, mainly domestic maltings which supplied the requirements for malt of the local population, many of whom brewed at home for their own consumption and for employees working both inside and outside. The actual brewing work was carried out normally by women and sometimes supervised by farmers' wives, if not actually doing the work themselves.

The expansion of British towns and cities in the 17th and 18th centuries, but especially London, encouraged the London brewers, using malt obtained from Hertfordshire and North-west Essex to expand their brewing capacity to satisfy the ever-growing demand for strong beer. It was this expanding beer market that was at the very heart of the malt production with which this chapter is concerned, and its importance must be stressed. By 1754, 85% of the malt produced in Saffron Walden was sent to London.[4] The remaining 15% was used locally by common brewers, inn keepers still brewing their own beer, and home brewers, the latter group remaining important until the second half of the 19th century.

Brewing and beer consumption was seen as being patriotic. Strong beer was drunk by males and small beer by families and their servants. Reformers such as William Cobbett and others were hostile to the introduction of tea drinking as a replacement for beer. He wrote: 'I view the tea drinking as a destroyer of health, an enfeebler of the frame, an engender of effeminacy and laziness, a debaucher of youth and a maker of misery for old age' and much more besides.[5] The temperance movement and the Quakers were also supportive of the malting and brewing industries.

Malting has always been an industry located in the barley growing areas where the by-products of the process could be sold back to farmers as animal feedstuffs (malt culms consist of dried sproutlets and rootlets from the malt) and malt dust as a fertiliser. The malt, of two basic brewing types, brown and pale, was then transported to the brewer (or the distiller who also used malt) located many miles away, usually in an urban area, close to his market for the finished product, beer or ale.

Fig. 10. The Maltmaker by Jill Tweedie.

Until the 1970s, the British malting industry worked in weights and measures which were part of the Imperial Corn Measure. A Quarter, a measure of volume containing eight bushels, was the standard unit of measurement. A quarter of barley should weigh 448 lb, but a quarter of malt only 336 lb. This quarter of malt could produce between 80 and 100 lb of soluble material or brewers' extract. Clearly then, it was cheaper to transport the malt to the end user, the brewer, rather than the heavier unmalted barley.

The census returns of 1841-1891 do not always differentiate between the various categories of people engaged in malting. They were often described by the enumerator of the day simply as 'maltster', but many of those described thus were probably employed 'maltmakers' and some malting labourers. The statue (Fig. 10), unveiled in Ware in November 1999, to commemorate the Millennium, and the men who worked in the Ware malting industry from 1399-1994, shows a 'maltmaker' proudly holding his wooden shovel with the malting cat at his foot. The maltmaker was the highly skilled employee of the maltster proprietor and the key man in the malting. Much of the success of the North-west Essex and East Hertfordshire malting industry depended on these skilled craftsmen. Floor malting, before the scientific introductions of the 19th century, was a craft rather than an industrial process.

The North-west Essex malting industry was orientated towards the Hertfordshire marketing structure centred on Ware. The product became known as 'Ware Malt' and it was highly regarded by the London brewers and preferred in the 18th century to supplies from other areas. Ware, where the barges loaded for London, had a direct waterway connection to Bow Creek via the Lee Navigation and handled malt from Cambridgeshire and Bedfordshire as well as Hertfordshire and North-west Essex. Daniel Defoe wrote in 1724 that:

> The rest of Cambridgeshire [South of Ely] is almost wholly a Corn Country; and of that Corn five Parts in Six of all they sow is Barley which is generally sold to Ware and Royston and other great Malting Towns in Hertfordshire and is the Fund from whence that vast Quantity of Malt called Hertfordshire is made which is esteemed best in England.

Of the Roothings in Essex, he wrote:

> There are no less than ten towns almost together, called by the Name of Roding and is famous for good land, good Malt and dirty roads, the latter indeed in Winter are scarce passable for Horse or Man.[6]

The soil of the Roothings is consistent heavy chalky boulder clay, better suited to wheat than malting barley. In the early 18th century, when Defoe was writing, this distinction was less well understood and therefore of lesser importance than it later became as large areas of lighter soils in Norfolk and Suffolk, ideally suited for growing malting barley, were brought into intensive arable cultivation based on the new sheep and corn regimes.

Barley farming for malting

Barley has been cultivated from time immemorial and is believed to have been derived from wild grasses native to northern Africa and western Asia. The Egyptians, Romans and Danes all grew it before the Norman invasion of England. It is used for human consumption and has been an important cereal for bread in parts of Europe including England and especially Scotland. Secondly, and more importantly, its value as a safe animal feedstuff for all livestock remains a customary end use. However, the conversion of barley into malt, mainly for brewing, but also for distilling, has always been the most important market for the best and the very best of the barley crop. Approximately 70% is used for malting.

The cultivation of barley in the British Isles has a very long history and it has been widely grown under many varying soil and climatic conditions. Even high rainfall areas and heavy soils have produced some barley, much of which was converted into low grade malt for local use. As long as a barley will germinate, malt production is possible but of varying qualities often acceptable only to local brewers and domestic users. Prolonged wet harvests were likely to produce barley where germination had already commenced and thus it was useless for malting. High quality malting barley is most likely to be produced on lighter free-draining soils, overlying chalk in the low rainfall counties of eastern England and

Scotland. North-west Essex and East Hertfordshire provided these conditions, hence the well-established malting industry of Saffron Walden and other local towns including Royston, Bishops Stortford, Ware and Sawbridgeworth.

The characteristics looked for in high quality malting barley – apart from the essential one that it will germinate – are that it should be plump, thin-skinned, mealy and low in nitrogen. By contrast a poor sample will be thin, containing less starch, probably thick-skinned which produces no malt, and the grain will be hard and flinty which delays the malting process and produces less fermentable extract. Heavy clay soils tend to produce these unwanted characteristics and much of Essex is well known for heavy clay soils. Apart from North-west Essex, much good barley was produced in several areas where there were lighter soils and the Tendring Hundred, east of Colchester, was one such area famous for quality malting barley and it remains so to this day.

Before the advent of scientific agriculture in the 19th century, plant breeding as we know it today was not possible. The established source for seed improvement for generations had been by selection and it was believed that seed exchanged from grower to grower, and therefore grown on fresh ground, may improve the yields. Walter of Henley writing in the 13th century declared: 'Change your seed every Michaelmas, for seed grown on other ground will bring more profit than that which is grown on your own. Will you see to this? In the mid-17th century S. Hartlib wrote: 'It is excellent husbandry every year to change the species of graine, and also to buy your seed corne from places farre distant.'[7]

By the 18th century three main kinds of barley were being grown for malting. Firstly, an early ripener, which had the advantage of a short growing season and therefore was suitable for wetter soils which were sown late. Secondly, a 'middle-ripe', which was probably the origin of Chevallier barley which was still being grown in the late 19th century as it was favoured by both farmer and maltster. The third type was 'late-ripe', which demanded the best growing conditions on light soil, but produced the highest quality samples for malting.'[8]

The story of Chevallier barley development around 1820 is worth recounting. A farm labourer named John Andrews of Debenham, Suffolk, after a day's work threshing barley, found part of an ear of barley lodged in his boot. It appeared to be an outstanding specimen so he kept the seed and planted it in his garden. This he continued to do for a year or two and eventually he passed over some seed to his landlord, the Rev. John Chevallier. He then grew it on for some years and distributed seed amongst his farming neighbours. As Chevallier was not early ripening, it needed to be sown early in the year which indicated its suitability for light land. On heavier soils it tended to lodge (flatten or go down making harvest difficult).[9]

Agricultural improvement in the 18th century centred around the adoption by farmers of flexible crop rotations which included the growing of root crops, cultivated grass and clover. By growing these crops, more livestock could be kept and more land manured, soil fertility raised leading to higher yields of corn. On light land the old ways of two corn crops and a fallow year became obsolete. The new system became known as the Norfolk Four Course Rotation because a sequence of four crops was followed, alternating each year between corn or a fodder crop. The cropping then was, wheat followed by roots (turnips or swedes fed to sheep kept on arable land), and then barley under-sown with grass and clover or sainfoin and grazed, the following year cut and made into hay. The reason for explaining this advance towards intensification is that it was particularly important for the development of light land hitherto used only for rough grazing producing little else but some 'sheep feed'. By bringing into arable cultivation these sandy soils, often in Norfolk, Suffolk and Lincolnshire, the potential for malting barley growing on new land could be spectacular as yields per acre also rose.

These developments did not escape the notice of landowners and farmers who were possessed of the capital required for land reclamation and improvement. As these lands were inherently acid, expensive marling (spreading a mixture of clay and chalk dug from field pits) was necessary to correct the soil acidity before barley could be grown. Other capital outlay, such as hedging following enclosure, was also undertaken and new farms were built and roads constructed. A modern estimate is that some 4,000,000 acres were added to the national resource. Of great importance to the malting barley growers in the traditional growing areas of North-west Essex and East Hertfordshire, was the potential competition they would now face from fine quality uniform barleys coming onto the market which were of considerable interest to the London brewers. These same light land areas of the country in Norfolk, Suffolk and Lincolnshire remain to this day the premier sources of malting barley with the county of Norfolk considered by many to be, not only the earliest area, but the home of the best barley by which others are judged.

So important did Norfolk become to the malting trade in the 1820s that:

Evidently, Cromer at holiday in July and August became an informal congress of brewers, bankers, landowners and malt merchants, many of them linked by ties of kinship and all by a common concern with the barley harvest.[10]

Fig. 11. The former maltings at 17 High Street, Saffron Walden.

Amongst these people were members of the Taylor family, John and his son Joseph, who were prominent malt factors and maltsters of Bishops Stortford. In 1838 members of this family leased the maltings and brewery in Saffron Walden at 17 High Street (later Raynhams Garage) from the Gibson family of Saffron Walden. The building has recently been redeveloped for housing (Fig. 11).

History of malting

Malting is one of the oldest domestic, and later industrial, processes. The ancient Eygptians understood the craft of malting barley and produced a malted beverage which was the ordinary drink of the population. The Romans in Britain encouraged the process and produced early liquor laws. The Danes were great beer drinkers and encouraged alehouses but regulated their numbers. The monastic system favoured malting and brewing and the monks were well-known for the high quality of their ales.

An act passed in 1394 placed restrictions on the sale of malt from Huntingdon, Hertford, Bedford and Cambridge to London unless it was properly cleaned of dust and barley debris. Trade in malt made in these localities north of London, including North-west Essex, was to develop into the most important source of malt supplying the London brewers. Much of the malt made in North-west Essex was destined for delivery to London via Ware and later Bishops Stortford. By 1585, 26 London brewers were producing 648,000 barrels of beer per annum.[11]

In 1697 a malt tax was introduced which was to last for 183 years. Maltsters were required to pay this on all barley used for malting. The tax was introduced at the rate of 6¾d (± 2.5p) per bushel. There was some relief for private homes.[12] Due to the dispersed location of maltings in rural areas the excise officers faced some difficulty in collecting the duty, especially in winter when the roads were bad. It was generally recognised that duty avoidance was widely practiced. However, not until 1880 was the system changed, and additional duty raised on beer sales to compensate for the loss of malt duty, by which time the duty had risen to 2s 8d per bushel.[13]

Around 1722, in a brewhouse at Shoreditch in London, a new type of beer was brewed which was the first to be technically well suited to mass production, and became known as porter supposedly because it was much favoured by manual workers in London. This was at the time a very important and valuable development for the regional malting industry of Hertfordshire and North-west Essex. The new beer was black, bitter to the taste, and of great apparent strength. Today the nearest equivalent is stout. Its manufacture was dependent on brown malt for which the maltsters of this region were well respected suppliers of long standing. Most important was the fact that porter brewing was not dependent on malt produced from only the finest barleys – lesser quality malt could be used. As London continued to expand throughout the 18th century, the demand for brown malt for porter brewing increased to the benefit of all those involved in its production including the local maltsters and barley growers.[14]

Towards the end of the 18th century the London brewers began tentative moves to gain more control of their malt requirements by getting closer to the market. This began as a gradual process but very significant for the established malting industry of Hertfordshire and North-west Essex. Malt could now be shipped into London, coastwise, at very competitive rates. These competed directly with inland waterway rates to London via the Lee Navigation, and from 1768 from Bishops Stortford via the Stort Navigation link to the Lee. The brewers concluded that new maltings could be owned or hired in East Anglian coastal ports such as Yarmouth and Lowestoft, and with their help and influence the local maltsters could be persuaded to produce malt of a higher quality more suited to their requirements.

During this period Norfolk was expanding barley production and at the same time increasing the farm yields per acre of very high quality barley ideally suitable for making pale malt.

A further opportunity recognised by the brewers who owned or rented maltings, was their ability to test their buying efficiency through comparison with malt purchased on the open market.[16] It was the malt factor, as the middleman, who was the traditional commercial link between sales maltster and brewer. He arranged the finance for purchasing, quality evaluation and transport to the brewer. Although independent of the brewer, his livelihood was closely related to satisfying the brewers' requirements, and he had to watch his step as the following extract of a letter dated 23 March 1803 shows, from Hanbury, the London brewer, to John Taylor, malt factor of Bishops Stortford: 'I wish you to load Brown Malt not Malt Dust... if you cannot get a few screens in your country I will send some down'. And again on 13 September 1803:

> I have sent you by coach a sample of the last pale Malt you sent in, it is so infamously bad that I am surprised you could even let me have it. However, to prevent any further trouble I beg to inform you I will not receive another sack of it into my Brewhouse... should I have occasion ever to write such another letter I shall entirely alter my plan of buying.[17]

In January 1803 Hanbury, who had been caught out in a falling market, wrote that he (Taylor) should try and get his maltster to take one shilling off the price and 'do your best for me and for once learn to be the Brewers' not the Maltsters' Factor'.[18]

The process of greater integration by the London brewers hiring or owning their own maltings and using increasing quantities of 'Ship Malt', mainly from Norfolk, continued into the 19th century. It led to the long standing bond between the maltsters of Hertfordshire and North-west Essex in time becoming less secure as the realignment of brewers' requirements for malt favoured consignment from Norfolk to the disadvantage of their traditional suppliers.

Overall, the market for beer continued to expand as the population increased from 6 million to 14 million between 1722 and 1833. However, beer consumption per capita fell from one barrel per head to half a barrel per head per annum.[19] By 1830 there began a change in the pattern of demand as porter became less popular and was replaced by lighter pale ales. This shift in taste proved to be permanent and was not helpful to those maltsters specialising in brown malt. These lighter ales were made from pale malt which was the main output of the Norfolk maltings, and led to the strengthening of ties between the Norfolk maltsters and the London brewers established originally in the previous century. By the 1820s, for example, stocks of 'Ship Pale' (malt) in one London store were over 20,000 quarters, while pale malt from Hertfordshire was between 5,000 and 10,000 quarters. Brown malt from Hertfordshire was only 5,000 quarters.[20] Production of both pale and brown malt continued in the 19th century, with the emphasis shifting steadily towards pale malt. By 1840 Truman's alone were buying 48,000 quarters of malt from Norfolk and Suffolk, which by 1845 had increased to nearly 70,000 quarters. This amounted to 76% of their requirements.[21] Pale malts, of seemingly ever increasing quality, were proving to be, by the new scientific means of measurement, more cost-efficient than the traditional brown malt in spite of a somewhat higher initial price. After 1830, as the railways opened up the countryside, an increasing number of brewers began to make their own malt as purchases represented 65% of brewing costs. This exposed the sales maltsters to new competition. By

1862, according to the return of Maltsters' Licences, the number who also brewed had reached 39%.[22] It could be said that the brewer had become the maltster's greatest competitor.

Times were changing in other ways as from about 1800, the amount of malt used by private and institutional brewing decreased rapidly from about 50% of the total to only 19% by 1830 and fell still further to 5% by 1862. The brewers' consumption of malt increased correspondingly as their beers replaced the home-brewed variety. The spread of the railways led to the construction of new larger maltings where a railway connection could be made. Maltings were built locally at Newport, Stansted, Bishops Stortford and Sawbridgeworth (Fig. 12 – see also Fig. 13). It was not until 27 November 1865 that Saffron Walden was able to handle goods traffic on a branch-line from Audley End junction.[23]

During the years of agricultural depression commencing in 1879, when the wheat price tumbled, high quality malting barley still commanded a premium which for those farming on lightish land made just that difference that kept them solvent. The number of licensed maltsters in the UK fell from 13,358 in 1826, the highest number ever recorded, to 4,288 in 1879, that is a loss of 9,070 businesses in 53 years. However, despite this loss of businesses, malt production in the UK increased from 3.5 million quarters to 6.8 million quarters over the period 1826 to 1879. This was achieved by the construction of new multi-storied maltings with significantly enlarged capacity. The small traditional sales maltsters were increasingly being squeezed out.[24]

Figs. 12 & 13. Left - former maltings at Newport: the end gable logo reads 'Barnard Bros 1854'. The malt store at the far end is built next to the railway line. Right – former maltings in High Street, Manuden.

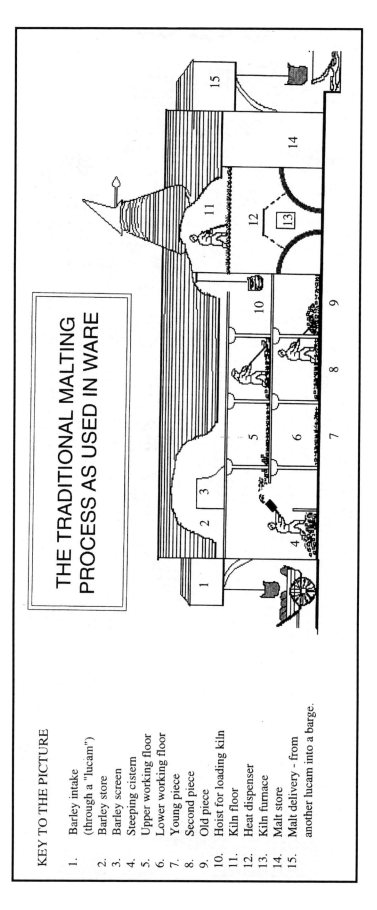

KEY TO THE PICTURE

1. Barley intake
   (through a "lucam")
2. Barley store
3. Barley screen
4. Steeping cistern
5. Upper working floor
6. Lower working floor
7. Young piece
8. Second piece
9. Old piece
10. Hoist for loading kiln
11. Kiln floor
12. Heat dispenser
13. Kiln furnace
14. Malt store
15. Malt delivery - from
    another lucam into a barge.

THE TRADITIONAL MALTING
PROCESS AS USED IN WARE

Fig. 14 – the floor malting process as used at Ware, but similar to that used in Saffron Walden maltings.

Part Two

By the early 18th century, Hertfordshire and North-west Essex were well established sources of good quality barley for malt-making. The process tended to be seasonal from October to May and thus labour could be hired after harvest and returned to the farm for haymaking in the following year.

The floor malting process

In technical terms malt is made from barley artificially germinated under controlled conditions. The germination is arrested by drying in order to conserve the saccharine or farinaceous matter in the grain which in brewing is turned into alcohol under the action of yeast fermentation. The process required considerable skill from the maltster and the use of only the better quality barleys which commanded a price premium in the market. To illustrate the floor malting process the Ware Museum have kindly supplied the illustration (Fig. 14), which follows the sequence of operations. The photograph taken at Dunmow Museum shows some of the tools used (Fig. 15). The wooden fork and shovel were used to turn barley on the growing floor, and the bushel measure is of galvanised steel with a lead government seal. On the right is the rake pulled through the barley on the granary floor and on the left a sack of malted grain.

Fig. 15. Some of the maltmaker's tools, on display at Dunmow Museum.

The barley harvest was usually completed by mid-September. Soon after, some of the threshed grain would be offered for sale, the price agreed and transport to the malting commenced. On arrival there, the grain was hoisted into the roof space via the overhanging lucam, one of the characteristic features of most maltings. Once in the roof space the grain was screened to remove extraneous matter and either stored for future use or immediately lowered to the steeping pit or cistern containing water where it remained for three or four days. These steeping pits were usually located on the ground floor and were of known capacity. During this process light unsuitable grain floating on the surface of the water would be skimmed off.

The next stage was couching which entailed removing the grain from the now-drained steep and allowing it to swell in a heap before it was placed into the wooden couch frame. The grain had by now swelled to its maximum and it was at this stage that the excise duty was calculated. The Excise Officer calculated the difference in volume between the grain in the steeping pit and the grain in the couch frame now that swelling was completed. Upon this calculation the excise duty or malt tax was to be paid within six weeks and long before the malt was sold.

From the couch the swollen grain was moved to the growing floor and spread no more than 12 inches deep. There the grain lay while germination proceeded but it was regularly turned with a wooden shovel or special rake to allow all parts to equally benefit from exposure to the air and to prevent the growing shoots from matting together. It was at this stage which lasted between 8 and 15 days, that the skill of the maltster and his maltmakers were most in evidence as they controlled the ventilation through the side windows, subject to weather conditions and exposure to air and light, which in turn determined the growth of the shoot. The London porter brewers were particularly concerned that this process was halted at the right time to maximise the saccharine content.[25] To halt the shoot growth the grain needed to be dried in the kiln which was at the far end of the growing floor. The germinated grain (green malt) was moved into the kiln and spread at a depth of 9-12 inches on wire screening, which was a later development in malt kilns and had replaced the woven hair-cloth used in earlier times. The grain remained in the kiln for 3-5 days while drying proceeded. The final type of malt and its colour was determined at this stage by the intensity of heat used and the duration of time in the kiln. The higher the temperature, the darker the colour – 130°F for pale malt which retained its barley colour and 180-300°F for brown malt, the speciality of Hertfordshire and North-west Essex and the type used by porter brewers in London.[26]

Up to *c.*1750 all kilns were fired with faggots or stackwood particularly favoured for the making of brown malt as it produced intense heat. Gradually 'Welch' coal and anthracite came into use in modified kilns as supplies of wood became more difficult to obtain. Smoke contamination was much feared as the malt became tainted. After kilning the dried malt was screened again to remove any shoots or rootlets (malt culms) and dust after which it was bagged and moved to the malt store where it was kept until required for dispatch to the brewery by whatever means were available.

This ancient process of floor malting was gradually superseded in the late 19th century by industrialised, semi-automated malting, sometimes built and owned by the breweries, often located in port areas with good railway connections.

Malthouse construction and development

Home and institutional brewing at the beginning of the 18th century used a very high proportion of the total malt produced. Between 1710 and 1719 beer made privately – that is beer made but not for sale – used roughly 65% of the malt produced. By 1810-19 this figure had reduced to around 45%.[27] By 1870 only 2.7% of beer was brewed privately, while the proportion made 'by common brewers' had risen from about 50% in 1830 to 95% in 1900'.[28]

To get some insight into the 65% of malt used in private brewing, a further examination of the probate inventories (mentioned earlier, compiled by F.W. Steer – see note 3) has been undertaken. Two parishes, Writtle and Roxwell in mid-Essex have been recorded for the period 1635-1749. They include all manner of household and farm-equipment, also livestock which had been valued for probate purposes. It therefore is an extremely valuable source from which to obtain this insight into the premises and equipment used for malting. Most of the malt kilns (kells) were on larger farms in the occupation of 'yeoman' farmers, as they were then described. In Roxwell parish four kilns are recorded and at Writtle seven: each except one had its haircloth, that is the horsehair mesh which allowed the heat from the kiln furnace to pass through, but also to support the drying green malt while in the kiln. At one location, Horsefrith Park in 1713 there was a 'wire' for the kiln - that was a wire mesh (a later development) instead of the more usual haircloth. This is a very early reference to wire-mesh being used for this purpose, but they later became common in commercial maltings. The kiln in most entries was associated with a malthouse or maltchamber, almost certainly a single storey, barn-like building which would incorporate the growing floor. 'Cisternes' or steeps are also mentioned into which the barley would be placed to soak to induce germination (there is a very early example of a floor level steep at Cressing Temple, Essex).

Fig. 16. Boyes Croft, Great Dunmow, now a malting museum.

Before brewing took place the malted barley had to be ground or milled. Just one mill came to light within the two parishes and that was at Duckes (farm), Roxwell where there were no less than 115 quarters of malt in a maltchamber valued at £115. This was evidently a commercial malting attached to the farm which had its own 'kell house' complete with a 'hayer' (haircloth). With only one mill, how then was the malt ground for brewing? Altogether in both parishes there were 23 malt quernes (quarnes) recorded of which only four were in premises where there was also a kiln. From this one must agree with F.W. Steer that many more people purchased malt for brewing than actually made malt themselves. Most villages, including locally Great and Little Chesterford, Clavering, and Manuden for example, at this time had their own small malthouse able to supply the local need for malt. Not many of these small malthouses survive today because they became redundant and were either demolished or converted into general storage buildings.

The next group of malthouses to look at are the town maltings. These supplied the local brewery and more distant markets in other towns, as well as selling malt locally for home brewing. Most of the older ones built in the 17th century have been replaced by more modern structures. That being so, it is very rare to find an example built in the 16th century which, with some modernisation, was still working in the 1940s. At Boyes Croft in Great Dunmow one can visit this unique building (Grade II*) which is open to the public and retains its structural and internal historical integrity (Fig. 16).

The oldest, timber-framed part, dates from the 16th century. It was built as a commercial seven-bay, timber-framed and part-brick malthouse, with two floors, under a clay-tiled roof. The steeping pit is contained within the two-storey brick and timber-framed building but above which is thought to have been a granary. There is a brick-built kiln with a conical clay-tiled replacement flue built in the 18th century, originally designed to burn faggots but converted to coal in 1890. The kiln floor is made of tensioned wire-mesh to support the drying green malt. Beyond the kiln is the malt store built in the 16th century where the finished product could be stored for several months prior to despatch. On the same site, to the west of the malthouse, is a pyramidal kiln probably used to dry damp barley. The output of Boyes Croft malthouse is thought to have been about 300-400 quarters per annum which is modest when compared with later buildings. Malt houses of this age are extremely rare compared with later examples, and the retention of its historical integrity is a great credit to everyone involved in its preservation in the face of pressures to demolish it and redevelop the site.

In the 17th and 18th centuries, town maltings continued to be built locally with timber framing as this was the traditional method of construction. One such can be seen through the archway behind number 23 Gold Street in Saffron Walden. There was, maybe, some brick used at lower levels. Unfortunately conversion to residential use has resulted in loss of its historical integrity. Another example of a small, early town malting can be seen behind the Eight Bells public house in Bridge Street, Saffron Walden, forming one side of the car park and now called the Barn Restaurant.

Timber became expensive and the industry turned to building in brick and locally just a few of these more substantial buildings survive in modified form and use, but not so easily recognised as being malthouses. Much of the production of three local brickworks was taken up by building new maltings. One probable 19th century example in Saffron Walden, is fairly easily recognisable as a malthouse. Now it is used as the School of Dance in Central Arcade, just off the High Street where the brick side wall can be seen complete with its rows of ventilating windows. Further afield a very fine malthouse is to be seen at Station Road, Newport. This building has been graded as being of both regional and national importance. It was built in 1853/4 by Barnard Bros adjacent to the railway line to facilitate transport. Three storeys high, with two conical slate covered kiln flues, it makes an impressive sight (see above, Fig. 12). At Bishops Stortford, adjacent to the Stort Navigation one can see a group of part brick, part timber malthouses known as Millars 1 and 2 near Southmill. Millars 3 on the same site, built in 1894, a massive construction with two pyramidal kiln flues, was the last of the floor malting types. Many brick-built maltings, now converted to other uses, have survived at Ware. Writing in 1885, H. Stopes, engineer and malting consultant, gave some further interesting information about what he termed 'the English Malthouse – Old Plan'.[29]

Malthouses of this plan are very rarely built of a size smaller than what is technically called a 15 quarter steep i.e. they steep or wet every 3½ to 4 days, 15 quarters of grain which gives a capacity of 120 quarters per month of malt made. As houses of this character usually work for only seven or eight months, then total capacity falls short of 1000 quarters per annum'. (Boyes Croft 300-400). The House should be of strong construction and consist of two floors or, if space is limited, of three floors and a kiln. The shape and size is ruled by the position of the house and site. The length of the growing floor should always exceed the breadth by at least 2/1. The capacity of the growing floor is the true gauge of the power of the malthouse and every measurement of all other parts should be calculated solely upon such capacity. A 75 quarter house is the largest that can be properly worked upon the English system unless of three growing floors although some of much greater capacity and size are working with results that are supposed to be satisfactory. The capacity of such a house is 5000 quarters per season.

There was much more of a technical nature to follow but one is left with the impression he did not approve of very, very large maltings as the quality of the product may be endangered.

Saffron Walden and area

Fig. 17. The malthouse behind 23 Gold Street, Saffron Walden, now converted for residential use, one of the few still existing in the town.

A visitor to Saffron Walden today may be surprised to learn that the town, during the 18th and earlier part of the 19th century, was the premier malting centre in Essex. For the casual visitor little remains to be seen of its former glory as a malting town. The industry developed over the previous 300 years. In 1600 the town had six malthouses and a manorial malt-mill in the market place.[30] By 1754 the area produced 13,970 quarters (2,095 tons) of malt which would represent the annual production from about 14 malt houses, not all of which were necessarily in the town itself as production from several outlying village maltings may be included. The industry continued to expand and by 1790 there were 22 malthouses in the town and by 1831 the total was 33 which would seem to be the highest number ever recorded.[31] The 1877 Ordnance Survey map of Saffron Walden shows the location of many of these maltings.

Maltsters recorded in *Pigots Directory* for 1823 and 1832 were respectively only 12 and 15. Those listed by Peaty (see note 31 above) for approximately the same period totalled 24 which is a more realistic number for 33 malthouses. Some maltsters probably operated more than one malthouse. They were widely scattered throughout the town but with a concentration in Gold Street including Powells Corner at the top (southern) end. There were at least seven in this area (Figs. 9, 17, 19, 20). The remaining 26, not all of which have been located, were to be found in Abbey Lane, Almshouse Lane, High Street (3), Myddelton Place, Bridge Street (2), Castle Street, Audley Road, Market Place, Hill Street and Church Walk.

Probably built later were those in the southern part of the town where, as mentioned previously, a railway connection was completed in 1865. These were located in Debden Road (Ross Lane), Station Street and close to the railway off West Road (Fig. 18).

Fig. 18. The pyramidal kiln is all that remains of the malthouse in Debden Road (Ross Lane) now called the Oast House.

The Castle Street malthouse and farm was owned by the Audley End Estate in September 1804 when the premises were described in a Sun Fire Office policy schedule, which shows the comprehensive range of buildings for the use of the tenant:

House and office adjoining in Castle Street tenant Thos Webb farmer £150. Malting office, Barley Chamber, Kiln, shop and Granary and adjoining near including the Kiln and Malting floors complete in every shape to receive the Malt for drying except the Cowel, Frame or hair cloth £200. Two stables, chaff house and cowhouse, cartlodge and Granary and Hay Barn adjoining £80. Corn Barn only near, thatched £100. All timber and tiled as above.[32]

The site of this farm and malting was a little to the east of Lower Square later redeveloped for housing and now known as Bellingham Buildings.

The Gibson family, who were of Quaker stock, arrived in Saffron Walden from Maldon in 1763 and opened a shop in Market Place. The family became prominent in malting and brewing in the late 18th and early 19th century. At the time there was no improper connection between brewing and Quaker religious beliefs and several London brewers were also members of the Society of Friends. In the later 18th century the family became the owners of the Anchor Brewery and maltings at 17 High Street and carried out a major refurbishment there in 1805. This site later became known as Raynham's Garage. Around 1838 it was leased to members of the Taylor family of Bishops Stortford. At one time the Gibsons owned a total of five maltings, 75% of the pubs and taverns in Walden and had an estate of 70 tied houses in East Anglia.[33] In addition to all these activities they owned several farms at Little Walden and had more land south of the town. Brewing and banking were never far apart and, as is well-known, the Gibson family opened the bank in Market Place, later to become Barclays. Over the years the family were great benefactors to the town in many different ways.

Figs. 19 & 20. An example of a successful maltings conversion can be found at 23 Gold Street, Saffron Walden. The left-hand picture shows the old maltings before conversion and the picture opposite shows the same scene afterwards.

Malt is a relatively high bulk, low value product where transport costs to the end user are always going to be a major factor in the cost structure. Production areas with good, low-cost transport facilities such as a canal or coastal seaport are always at an economic advantage over those dependent on more costly road transport.

In the case of Saffron Walden the route out for most malt lay to the south towards London via the Hockerill Highway (Harlow Bush to Stump Cross) turnpiked from 1744. Prior to this much malt was taken direct to Ware across country through Wicken Bonhunt, to join the London-Cambridge Road north of the town. This was a busy route as all the malt from Cambridgeshire and north Hertfordshire used it to reach the barge terminal at Ware where loading took place for London.

The proposal for the construction of a canal from Bishops Stortford to Saffron Walden and northward to Cambridge was considered once again at a public meeting held on 5 September 1768, at the Crown Inn, Great Chesterford, all earlier attempts having failed. The meeting was under the chairmanship of Richard Clark Esq., Alderman of the City of London. The proposal in favour of construction focussed on the needless gross waste involved in road transport caused by excessive use of horses and the costs involved. The results of a survey carried out showed that 154 stage wagons hauled by 871 horses had passed through Stamford Hill gate. As only three-quarters of a ton per horse was permitted by Parliament the total transported was 624 tons. This could have been carried in 16 barges hauled by just 16 horses, each barge loaded with 40 tons of cargo. The potential quantities of malt and barley to be transported were respectively 55,000 quarters (8,250 tons) and 10,000 quarters (2,000 tons) with a further 4,800 tons of mixed cargo.[34]

As with the earlier proposals for the construction of a canal which crossed the Audley End Estate there was a resounding protest and refusal by Lord Howard, 1st Lord Braybrooke. He was not alone and other objectors such as mill owners on the Cam or Granta feared loss of water to drive their mills and some farmers were concerned that their water meadows could no longer be flooded. It seems unlikely that road wagon owners, who were engaged in transporting the loads to Bishops Stortford and Ware, would have given their support. So, once again the proposals were shelved. However, in 1812, agreement was reached, a Bill passed, and the son of the 2nd Lord Braybrooke, Hon. Richard Neville, later the 3rd Lord Braybrooke was to be a director of a new canal company.[35] Work was not to commence until £425,000 of the total cost of £870,000 had been raised, which in the event was never forthcoming by the backers and so the prospect of a canal to connect Saffron Walden to Bishops Stortford and Ware died and was never revived (see also Chapter 6).[36]

In spite of this setback the malting industry in Saffron Walden continued to expand in the first part of the 19th century but the longer term prospects were not good. The arrival of the railway in 1865 probably helped to sustain the industry but it is significant that the later 19th century developments of large maltings in Essex took place where good transport connections existed or could be developed along the line of rail and at sea ports or river sites.

The malting industry after 1880

The year 1880 was a watershed for the malting industry because the Malt Tax Act, which had been in existence since 1697, was repealed by the Gladstone government. To compensate for the fiscal loss, beer duty was raised by 6s 3d on each standard barrel. As the malt tax had been levied across the board at a flat rate, malt produced from the highest quality barley with the highest extraction rate had been generally preferred to lower grades. This distinction now became of lesser importance and it was hoped that more second-grade barley, which was especially suitable for brown malt, would be purchased from English farms. This would have pleased many local growers farming on heavier, marginal malting barley land. This did not materialise as lower grade barleys were now being imported at low, cost-effective prices. By 1880 some 10% of barley used for malting was foreign and this increased to 43% ten years later. Shipments arrived from California, Chile, Persia and India as well as other countries. By 1902 Taylors of Hertfordshire, by now the most important regional maltster, was using 32% imported barley and this percentage was to increase in the following years.[37] The price of English barley for malting tumbled to around 22s 11d per quarter in 1896 from a high of over 40 shillings back in 1873.[38] Malt prices also fell in the same period and were only 27s 6d per quarter in 1896, having been 59s 6d in 1873.[39] These later years of the 19th century saw the commencement of a very long period of agricultural depression relieved only temporarily by the First World War. Barley – to some extent less exposed to foreign competition than wheat – remained at very low prices made worse by a series of wet harvests around 1879-80. Many cereal growers, especially those on heavy land were brought near to bankruptcy.

After 1880 the number of brewers fell from 2,162 to 1,111 by 1913 and many of them were producing up to 50% of their own malt requirements. They concentrated on the highest grades leaving some sales maltsters to produce the less profitable lower grades.[40] By now malt was subject to closer contract terms as the brewers' chemists measured more accurately the extract content. They also demanded more favourable delivery terms and moved towards those maltsters able to deliver huge quantities under a single contract. All this put extra pressure on the smaller sales maltsters.

To meet these new standards there was increased building activity to construct new multi-story maltings with a minimum capacity of 75-120 quarters producing 5,000-8,500 quarters per season. At ports and railheads even larger ones were built with five or six storeys and a capacity of 300 quarters producing 20,000 quarters per season. In 1906 at Sleaford in Lincolnshire a gigantic malting with a 1,000 feet frontage of six storeys and producing 60,000 quarters per season was completed. The days of the small sales maltster were surely numbered. Within this region at Sawbridgeworth, Bishops Stortford and Ware new multi-storey maltings were built but sadly not in Saffron Walden.

In spite of all these major developments elsewhere, malting in Saffron Walden continued in the traditional way up to the 1960s. In a recent conversation with a Great Sampford farmer, the writer was told that in the later 1940s, as a young boy, he assisted with transporting faggots from Clay Wood in Wimbish parish to the maltings in Station Road and the High Street/Gold Street maltings in Saffron Walden. These faggots were heavy and contained much thick wood and had to be of a specific and similar size. Evidently not every malting had been converted to coal burning and they were probably still producing brown malt in the traditional manner.

Brown malt is no longer made but the Greencore Malting Group today produce no less than eight different malts in total with their Bury St Edmunds malting producing 'Ale' and 'Pilsen'. Six coloured malts are produced in Yorkshire the names of which are 'Black', 'Chocolate', 'Roast Barley', 'Carpils', 'Crystal' and 'Amber', all required for a variety of beers and ales.

6

A Canal for Saffron Walden?

During the late 18th and early 19th centuries, three proposals were put forward to extend the canal system from Bishops Stortford northward to Saffron Walden and beyond in the general direction of Cambridge and the Great Ouse. These proposals were dated approximately 1777/80, 1789/90 and 1811/12.[1] This chapter   is concerned with plans presented in 1789 which, had they been implemented, would have had a major effect on the western part of the town. Unlike the 1777/80 design, which followed the valley of the Cam in front of Audley End mansion and would not directly connect with Saffron Walden town itself, this new proposal in 1789 brought the canal to near the town centre.

The Stort Navigation linking Bishops Stortford to Ware had been opened for traffic in 1769 and was fully operational in 1789. An extension northward would provide the maltsters, grain traders, and other merchants of Saffron Walden with cheaper transport to Bishops Stortford and to the barge terminal at Ware *en route* to London, thus avoiding a long and costly road journey. The general line of this proposed canal was established by survey in the winter of 1789, carried out by John Rennie, the foremost builder of canals in England at the time, and one of the first British civil engineers.[2] From this survey a map was prepared, a copy of which is now in the Essex Record Office (ERO D/DBy P4). This was a very major development proposal which, had it been constructed, would have linked London to the Great Ouse and to Kings Lynn and the Wash. This map has the following heading:

> A plan shewing the line of the Proposed Navigation From Bishop's Stortford through part of Essex, Cambridgeshire and Suffolk, to the Brandon River on the borders of Norfolk; approved by the General Meeting of the Noblemen, Clergy, Gentlemen & Freeholders of the said counties, Held at Great Chesterford in the year 1789 & Engraved by Order of The Honourable The City of London. Surveyed by John Rennie Engineer & F.R.S.E. London, Engraved & Published by Wm Faden Geographer to the King March 8th 1790.

As this map is far too large for publication, a description of it will be useful. The line of the canal touches the following places starting from Bishops Stortford town. Elsenham (tunnel 6 furlongs 1 chain), Newport, Saffron Walden (2 tunnels: 2 furlongs & 9 chains, and 4 furlongs & 1 chain), Littlebury, Little Chesterford, Great Chesterford (branch canal to Cambridge), Hinxton, Bourne Bridge (near Great/Little Abington), Six Mile Bottom, Lakenheath Lode on the river Brand near Wilton Ferry. There were to be reservoirs at Elsenham, Little Henham, Wicken Bonhunt and Linton. The meeting referred to in the map heading was held at the *Crown Inn*, Great Chesterford, now the *Crown House Hotel* and Restaurant. There is however a further small sketch map, 18 by 11 inches (an engraving of which belongs to the author), also in the Essex Record Office, which although undated shows in more detail the line of the canal from Sparrows End (today roughly the junction of the B1052 and the B1383 near Wendens Ambo as it was at that time), and north to the turn-off to Littlebury on the present B184, Windmill Hill to Stump Cross road (Fig. 21).[3] The purpose of this sketch map is unclear, but it may have been drawn in an effort to persuade Lord Howard, 1st Lord Braybrooke, to allow the canal to cross his land, a plan to which he had so vehemently objected in the past. It was this proposed new line through Saffron Walden that had implications for the town as we know it today.

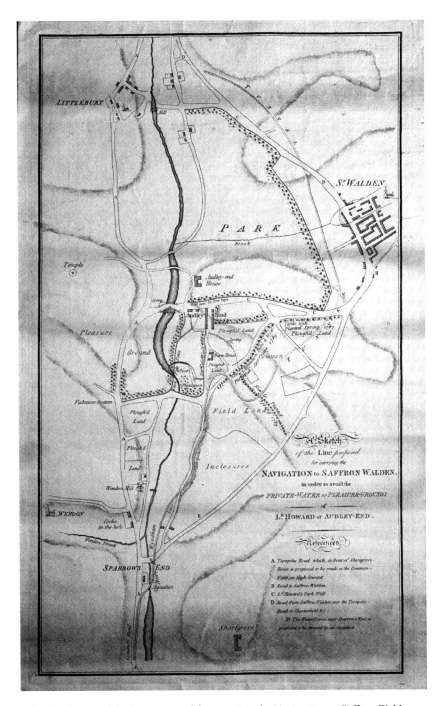

Fig. 21. The sketch map of the line proposed for carrying the Navigation to Saffron Walden.

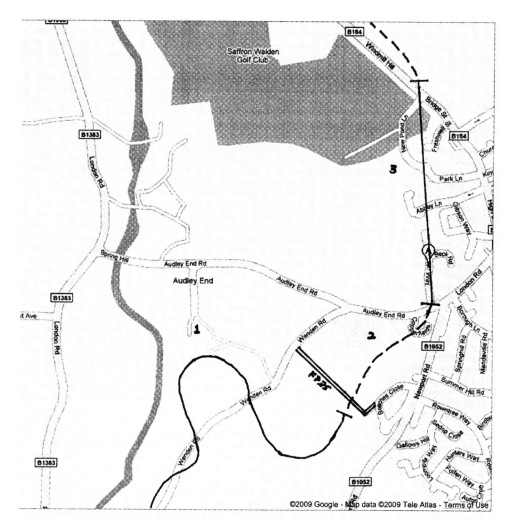

Fig. 22. The thick black line indicates where the proposed canal would have been in relation to modern streets of Saffron Walden and district. The broken black line shows where the canal would have been routed through tunnels.

In order to comprehend these implications, had construction gone ahead see Fig. 22, a present-day Google-map overlain with the canal's proposed route. A good view of the proposed line south of the town can be seen from the public right-of-way (FP 35, inserted on the map). It passes close to Abbey Farm approximately following the 60-metre contour and crosses over Beechy Ride before entering a tunnel. There were to be two of these to avoid the highest ground. This one south of the town passes under what are now the County High School playing fields and the Copperfields housing development fronting on to the Audley End Road, before emerging into the open again at the top of Saxon Way. The second tunnel to the north of the town would pass under Windmill Hill to the east of the road and emerge on the lower ground before the turn-off to Littlebury. The length of the southern tunnel was to be 2 furlongs & 9 chains (638 yards or 583.38 metres) and the northern one 4 furlongs & 1 chain (902 yards or 824.77 metres).

The line of the canal between the two tunnels was to be on the surface but, as there are substantial differences in height - some 55 feet (16.76 metres) between the top end of Saxon Way and the land around what is now Swan Meadow car park - a series of pound locks, not shown on the maps would have been required. On the northern side of the town, further locks may have been necessary to reach the level of the northern tunnel entry point, now part of the golf course car park and clubhouse site. Both tunnels would of course have been level.

Reference to the modern map shows the line approximately following Saxon Way and the footpath alongside the Battle Ditches to the Almshouses, passing them on the western side where Hanover Housing has now been built; thence over the low-lying land to Swan Meadow. Around this area a canal basin would have been constructed to incorporate warehousing, offices, loading and unloading facilities, stables and possibly some housing and bothies for bargemen. It would have been a very busy complex, but ideally situated for easy access from the town centre.

Alas, Lord Howard would not give way and the whole project had to be abandoned. This would have been a major engineering project and a boost to the economy of Saffron Walden with its malting trade. The total distance from Bishop's Stortford to Wilton Ferry on the river Brand, which was linked to the Little Ouse, was just over 52 miles.

A further proposal for a canal was considered and approved by all concerned in 1812, 15 years after the death of Lord Howard. In the event nothing came of this either, as the finance to commence construction was never forthcoming. All the land within the town has now been put to other uses, as we see today.

It is interesting to speculate now whether the canal with its tunnels could have survived to the present day, when its amenity and leisure value would surely have been appreciated and money found for restoration and maintenance. Many former navigations, some in Essex, are already being cared for as their amenity value seems worthwhile for recreational uses.

7

The Wool Industry of North-west Essex

Introduction

This chapter sets out to look at the production of wool in North-west Essex from 1086 to a period in the 18th century, after which wool was no longer the primary purpose of sheep husbandry. It draws upon the work of many experts who have written on the history of British wool and sheep husbandry. The towns of North-west Essex including Walden never achieved the prominence and reputation of Colchester, Braintree and Coggeshall for the manufacture of high-grade woollen cloth. According to the aulnagers' accounts for 1394-98, nine capitalist manufacturers, centuries before the introduction of machinery, were together producing 36,500 narrow cloths (about one yard wide) at Braintree and Coggeshall each year. At that time Colchester was the first town in England to be settled by Flemish weavers and later became the centre of 'New Draperies' manufactures. Essex cloth production was on a larger scale than Suffolk where numerous small manufacturers operated. However, during the development of major centres in Essex, weaving in Saffron Walden and in the surrounding towns and rural parishes was carried on as a largely cottage-based industry with sufficient capacity to satisfy local needs with some surplus for other markets.

I have divided this lengthy time-span into three periods, each of which ended in events which not only brought about changes in society but also had major implications for agricultural activities, the principal source at this time of all raw materials for industry including the economically extremely important production of wool. Without fine wool the history of Britain may have been quite different and it would be difficult to overstate the importance of wool exports and subsequently of cloth exports during the Middle Ages and the Tudor period. These two commodities were far and away the most valuable part of the export trade. Between 1303 and 1311 the annual value of wool exports alone, averaged £335,000 per year and did not fall below £323,000 up to 1336. For the time these were enormous figures.

Fig. 23. A Norfolk Horn ewe and her lamb, noted for fine short staple wool and probably the most popular breed in 18th century Essex. Some of the last few were kept at Littlebury Green in the 1950s. It is now a Rare Breed.

At the time of the Black Death in 1348/9 wool production declined but exports soon rose again between 1350 and 1360 to an all-time high of over £450,000 per year. In 1337 Edward III attempted to ban the export of raw wool and to encourage instead exports of finished cloth. Although his strategy failed, cloth exports did very slowly increase using the wool that had previously been exported.

Sheep raising for wool was widespread (Fig. 23). The 33,000 sacks of wool (a wool sack weighs 364 lbs) exported in the 1330s, took the wool of 8,580,000 sheep. On this basis it took the fleeces of about 260 sheep to fill one sack. There are no figures for the size of the home market but it must have been considerable, raising the likely numbers of sheep to well over nine million. Some calculations have shown this number to be minimal.[1]

Edward I imposed a tax on wool exports of 6s 8d per sack in 1275 and in 1313 Edward II set up a staple in St Omer. During 1353 Parliament passed The Statute of Staples to ease the task of collecting duties and to regulate the trade by enforcing the marketing of all wool, of which there were 44 different grades, through designated towns and exported only by authorized merchants known as 'Merchants of the Staple'. The staple towns in East Anglia were Norwich, Ipswich, Yarmouth and Lynn. In 1363 the foreign staple was removed first to Bruges but later to Calais, these both being centres closely connected with the manufacture of finished cloth. The English cloth trade grew in the 14th century while raw wool exports declined and by 1450 only 8,000 sacks were exported and by 1600 this had dwindled to a mere 150 sacks.[2]

Wool and cloth manufacture were the first branch of industry to be brought under national control. It was not to be left to the uncertain fortunes of traders, as it was too important for that. Elaborate statutes were introduced for its protection and to guard against misfortunes.

Finally in this introduction, a short poem extolling the virtues of the humble sheep written by Leonard Maxwell in 1662:

These Cattle sheep amongst the rest,
Is counted for man one of the best,
No harmful beast, no hurt at all,
His fleece of wool doth cloath us all,
Which keeps us all from extreme cold;
His flesh doth feed both young and old;
His tallow makes candles white,
To burn and serve us day and night,
His skin doth pleasure divers waies,
To write, to wear, at all assaies,
His guts thereof we make wheel strings
They use his bones for other things,
His horns some shepherds will not lose
Because therewith they patch their shoes:
His dung is chief I understand
To help and dung the Plowman's Land:
Therefore the sheep among the rest,
He is for man a worthy beast.

Part 1: Domesday Survey to the Black Death: 1086-1348/9

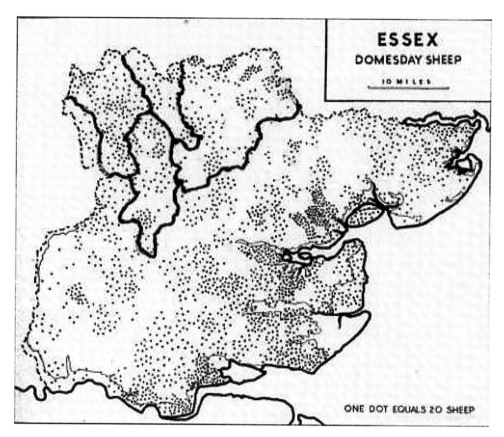

Fig. 24. Domesday sheep on Essex demesne 1086 (boundaries of the five North-west Essex hundreds added by author).

The Domesday Survey of Essex taken in 1086 is an important and appropriate starting point from which to begin a study of the wool industry with particular focus on the five hundreds of North-west Essex (Fig. 24). These are Dunmow, Clavering, Uttlesford, Freshwell and Hinckford.

   The part of the survey that records livestock numbers counts only those animals kept on demesne land (land normally owned by seigniorial estates) such as abbeys and lay manorial estates. No records exist of the livestock owned by peasants which are thought to have been considerable. The total number of sheep recorded in Essex was 46,000 of which 18,000, the largest concentration, were grazed on the south Essex marshes. They were kept primarily to produce milk for cheese and butter, only secondly for wool. At that time ewes were considered to be the main dairy animal and all milking and dairy work was performed by women (Fig. 25).

The next highest density of sheep was recorded in the five north-west hundreds listed above. Approximately 3,700-4,000 were kept in this predominantly arable farming part of the county, which had a higher density of plough teams and ploughs than anywhere else in Essex. We tend to think of sheep as a grassland grazer of the wide open spaces such as the south Essex marshes, but this was not so in North-west Essex where the sheep were an integral part of an arable farming system, kept mainly for their wool but of equal or even greater importance for the maintenance of soil fertility on the arable land.[3]

Fig. 25. Milking and salving sheep, from the Luttrell Psalter (c.1340).

The sheep-fold system was widespread in medieval times, the sheep grazing by day on the stubbles, headlands, manorial waste and common grazing, but folded (restricted within a hurdled enclosure) at night on the arable land. The value of this practice for its contribution to soil fertility was recognised in medieval times and confirmed by the detailed regulation of it by manorial instruction. The sheep were thus acting as transporters of nutrients from the daytime grazing to the arable land on which they were folded at night. The folds were moved from time to time across the arable land so that there was an even distribution of nutrients to every part.

Grazing land in North-west Essex was always in short supply and became less so as new assarts (land clearances) were made. A system of stinting (numerical control of the numbers of livestock allowed on common grazing) was employed by manorial authorities. In addition to this grazing, always supervised by a shepherd with his dog, were the long corn stubbles left after harvest and before they were ploughed. In the common three-course rotation of those times only land coming into winter wheat or rye would be ploughed before Christmas, the remainder left as sheep grazing of a sort, however poor, which included the land destined for a restorative fallow. Sheep were sometimes housed in bad weather in sheepcotes (sheephouses) well strewed with straw, where they were protected and could receive additional food (Fig. 26). One location of a sheepcote was at Sheepcote Green, Clavering and there were others in North-west Essex.

Much of what was written about medieval sheep husbandry came from the pen of Walter of Henley in *His Husbandry*, the earliest known work on this subject thought to have been written in the 13th century. Walter gained his experience while working as a bailiff, an important and responsible position on large estates. Another source of information is *The Office of Seneschal* (the steward, a step above bailiff), the author of which is unknown. This work gives advice on estate management and appears to be also 'written' in the 13th century.[4]

The origins of British sheep are obscure but it is generally thought that the feral, naturally short tailed Soay sheep harbours the descendants of the Bronze Age animals kept mainly for milk and meat. Their coats were coloured rather than white and consisted of a mixture of wool and hair. This hair is known as 'kemp'. Today this type is kept only as a Rare Breed. It was not until after the Roman occupation that British sheep fleeces became whiter and woollier due probably to the introduction of sheep from southern Europe. These new sheep were born with long tails, as all modern sheep have, which for hygiene reasons are docked soon after birth. Their wool was not necessarily finer (fine woolled sheep cost most) but any wool could be used for weaving into coarse cloth much in demand by poorer people.

Fig. 26. A medieval sheepcote with the flock housed inside to protect them from the weather.

From these early beginnings the large range of British sheep types emerged gradually by a process of selection and probably further importation. The larger flock masters travelled great distances to find improved sheep with fine fleeces to stock their demesne farms. A big trade developed in improved fine woolled sheep to stock the new Cistercian foundations in the north of England.[5]

The question of who owned the sheep in North-west Essex is an important one. All sheep owners were committed to the production of wool before any other consideration. The owners of the largest flocks were the two abbeys, Walden and Tilty. The priory of Ely, a major sheep owning Benedictine foundation, had substantial numbers at Littlebury and possibly at Hadstock as well. In addition to these there were smaller ecclesiastical establishments no doubt keeping small flocks. The principle lay establishment would have been the Manor of Walden with its manor house located at the castle site in the town. Their tenants would also have kept sheep with flocks of six sheep upwards to several hundreds.

The Benedictine abbey at Brook Walden which would have followed traditional feudal, mainly arable farming practices, had been established as a priory in 1136, but was elevated to an abbey in 1190. The Book of the Foundation speaks of an assart of 120 acres which formed the nucleus of the demesne and there was a further 100 acres cleared at the secondary manor of St Aylotts.

There are unfortunately no records of the sheep kept in the 12th century. Benedictine establishments in the period before the Black Death disaster relied upon customary labour required to fulfil their quotas of labour services in return for the tenancy of land. As direct tenants they were not allowed to keep sheep but could keep other stock, no doubt mainly draught oxen, required for ploughing their own land and for work on the demesne.[6]

The Cistercian abbey of Tilty was established in 1153 on land between Dunmow and Thaxted on the river Chelmer. The Cistercians devoted their energies to labour and industry and chose settlement sites in remote areas. They employed no servile customary labour, but instead had lay-brothers within their community who carried out all the work on their demesnes. The order were famous for their agricultural skills, especially sheep farming and the wool they produced was normally of the highest quality and fine enough to attract buyers from Flanders and Italy. The price schedules for wool sold in the 13th century illustrates the marked dominance held by the Cistercians for wool coming from their abbeys, including Tilty and two others in Essex namely Coggeshall and Stratford Langthorpe. Forty-one Cistercian abbeys in England supplied 80% of the export volume whereas Benedictine abbeys only supplied 2%. Wool from the Essex Cistercian abbeys averaged just over the high price of £11 per sack. It is thought that the reason for this high price was that the Cistercians only sold 'prepared' rather than raw unsorted wool. The highest price for wool at the time was over £18 per sack originating in Herefordshire from Cistercian houses there.

Much of the lower grade wool from Essex was exported to Scandinavia being not good enough for the weavers of Flanders or Italy. Tilty Abbey owned granges (demesne farms) at Bardfield, Waltham, Radwinter, Chigwell and Fakenham. At Coggeshall their very magnificent grain barn is now owned by the National Trust and is open to the public, a reflection of the Cistercian commitment to agriculture. The late John Hunter referred to Tilty Abbey as 'a serious agribusiness' which, like most Cistercian abbeys, indeed it was.[7,8]

The priory of Ely mentioned above was soon after 1108 incorporated into the new bishopric and from that time the demesne estates were vested in the bishop. It is recorded that in 1251 the foundation owned 10,500 acres in Essex and Hertfordshire divided into three categories of use, namely demesnes, villeinage and rent paying tenancies, each category having approximately 3,500 acres. They owned extensive lands in other counties as well and kept an estimated 9,000 sheep, of which approximately 300 were on their lands in Littlebury. Their estate there extended to Littlebury Green and Catmere End. If the sheep owned by their dependent tenants were to be included, the total was probably about 13,000 on all the Bishop's estates.

The customary tenants at Littlebury – villeins and bordars – were required to fold their sheep on the lord's land to ensure maintenance of fertility. This was not an unusual burden placed upon customary tenants. Six named men, who were probably free tenants, who paid rent for their land were excluded from this requirement.[9,10] Customary tenants had access to various amounts of land on which to grow their subsistence crops but it is estimated that some 30% had under five acres, each of which would barely have provided sufficient grain to feed the average family.[11]

In 1348 the Black Death first appeared in England on the shores of Dorset and spread rapidly through the country resulting in the death, it is thought, of over 40% of the population. No group was spared. This horrific event continued intermittently for several more years.

The two most significant consequences that followed, especially for the rural population, were a shortage of labour to work on manorial farms and estates, and secondly very many vacant holdings resulting in uncultivated land lying idle. Customary servile tenants had had long standing grievances about the severity of their labour dues and had been demanding payment in cash in return for their labour. This movement was to gain momentum as manorial lords faced the difficulties brought about by labour shortages and uncultivated, abandoned land.

The solution arrived at reluctantly, was to lease out part of the demesnes and some previously tenanted land to enterprising peasants who were prepared to take risks with long leases and thus free themselves from servile ties. This saw the beginning of a new class of often young tenants, who were for generations to come to be the nucleus of British farming stock.

The second consequence resulting from the Black Death was the laying down to grass of former arable land and increased concentration on sheep husbandry for wool production which involved a far lower labour requirement than arable farming.

Part 2: Black Death to Dissolution of the Monasteries: 1349-1538

The second half of the 14th century was a period of economic upheaval with intermittent outbreaks of the Black Death from 1348/9 followed by the Peasants Revolt in 1381. Both events contributed to the breakdown of the old manorial rural organisation based upon unpaid labour services in return for land.

However in Clavering, Thaxted and at Pounces manor, Walden all labour services had been commuted to rent or leases by 1345, according to the historian John Hunter. The wool industry both nationally and in Essex expanded rapidly with London and Colchester becoming major wool exporting ports. By 1355 England was shipping 40,000 sacks annually, most wool from west Essex being exported through London. The trade was however not just one way, and during this period England imported an average 6,000 cloths per year woven in Flanders, mainly from English wool. This was about to change.

Cloth manufacture in England was encouraged by government measures including for a short time a ban on the export of raw wool. Cloth manufacture grew rapidly and exports soon reached 20,000 per annum.[12] The increase in cloth production is generally thought to have occurred for two main reasons apart from any government legislation. Firstly, some Fleming weavers were invited in 1343 by Edward III to settle in England. They brought with them their weaving skills.

Secondly and more importantly was the construction in this period of fulling mills on rural streams which brought cloth manufacture to many new areas. Fulling mills pounded the wet cloth, at the same time removing the natural oil and tightening the weave. Prior to the advent of these special mills, this process was carried out by foot. When fulling was completed the cloth was hung out to dry on tenter frames suspended on the frame from 'tenter hooks', after which the cloth was ready for the finishing processes (Fig. 27).

Fig. 27. A modern tenter frame. The two rows of tenter hooks can be seen clearly on which the wet cloth, after fulling, is stretched and dried.

Fig. 28. The west end of the Woolstaplers' Hall, drawn shortly before demolition in 1848.

Fig. 29. Sketches of six carved heads on the hammer beams of the Woolstaplers' Hall.

In the early 14th century there is a record of Henri Darci, citizen and clothier of London and Overhall in Littlebury (Bordeaux Farm area today) having an interest in a water-mill, possibly one of the three recorded on the Cam.[13] According to the Cartulary of Walden Abbey there was a 'Fullymelle croft' with tenter frames owned by the Abbot of Walden on the Cam. Fulling and dyeing were complementary trades and some men appear to have been both fullers and dyers. At Newport there existed a tenter field at the junction of School Lane and Bury Water Lane which, although having been built over in recent times, retains the name Tenterfield. No doubt water for fulling was obtained from the Bury stream nearby.

Among the many centres of weaving in Essex between 1350 and 1500, 11 were situated in the five hundreds of North-west Essex. These centres were Birdbrook, Finchingfield, Sturmer, Canfield, High Easter, Takeley, Felsted, Clavering, Stebbing, Thaxted and Saffron Walden.[14] Much of the cloth made was to supply the needs of the local population and was of the cheaper variety known as 'kersies'. Some was also sent to London to supply an expanding market there. In 1300 some 23,000 miles of cloth was required to supply the home market. While England produced much wool of superb quality, that coming on to the home market for use by the general population was often not suitable for export and Essex, and much East Anglian wool was not highly regarded.

During the medieval period three methods were employed to bring wool from the producer to the clothier who largely financed and organised the whole operation and manufactured the cloth. Those with sufficient wealth would purchase their wool direct from the largest producers soon after shearing was completed and pay for it at that time. Secondly, those clothiers less well off would buy from a wool merchant or 'stapler' who was the middle-man between the producer and clothier. The third option, for those without sufficient ready funds, was to buy yarn from spinners who came to the market to sell what they had spun, having purchased small lots of wool from peasant producers. Wool for the export trade was sometimes purchased by foreign buyers, often Italians, who were accustomed to buying the whole clip from selected monastic establishments where the wool quality was what they wanted. Having bought the wool it was sorted, graded and re-packed for export.

Before leaving the subject of wool buying mention must be made of the importance of Stourbridge Fair (Sturbridge) at Cambridge set up by King John in 1211 and held each year on Stourbridge Common (Newmarket Road) in the autumn and lasting 20 days. Considered by Defoe in a later period to be the greatest fair in England, it was the meeting place where long staple wool from Lincolnshire was purchased by merchants from Essex, Suffolk and Norfolk to the value of £50-£60,000 each year. During the 15th century fairs declined in importance as towns expanded and could afford to build their own market halls.[15]

Chepyng Walden had its own Woolstaplers' Hall, built it was thought in the reign of Henry VII (1485-1509) just off Market Street (now King Street) and close to Cloth Row (Figs. 28 & 29). Along with other medieval buildings it was demolished in 1848 to make way for the Corn Exchange. Apparently it was during this demolition that the small hall was revealed. At some time when no longer used as a market hall it had been converted into a domestic habitation, presumably when the wool industry collapsed in the 18th century. From the illustration it was clearly a high quality building with a very fine hammer-beam roof. Its demolition was a considerable loss to the town.[16]

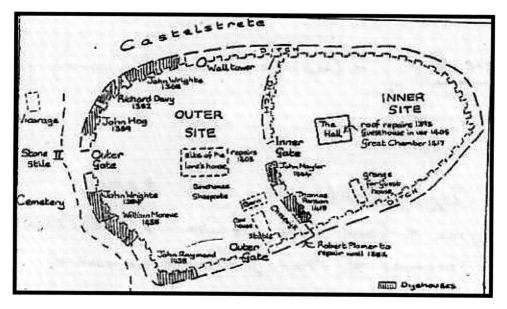

Fig. 30. Reconstruction of how the Castle Hill site at Walden may have looked in medieval times.

Although cloth manufacture in Chepyng Walden never became as important as it was in Braintree, Bocking, Coggeshall or Colchester, there is evidence of a number of dye-works situated within the site of Walden Castle, the earliest of which is confirmed as dating from 1359.[17] Between that date and 1454 Cromarty records eight entries in the Walden manor court rolls concerning dyers, a number of whom were described also as being fullers. They were leasing small plots of land, 4-8 perches (66-132 feet) long 'beneath the walls'. These records were often about infringements of various regulations or requests to re-build walls and so on.

This 'industrial' area became known as Taintershill, the general area being known as Berryhill. Water for dyeing was probably obtained from a well within the castle site, as local streams were too polluted to supply clean water. A possible lay-out is shown in Fig. 30, and the town layout in Fig. 31.

Although there is no evidence of a fulling mill in Chepyng Walden, it is interesting that around 1500 Park Lane in the town was called 'Fullers Lane' and close by were springs on 'Frosschwell Hundryd'. Dyes at this time were all derived from organic sources and although there were some 15 different types the most commonly used were woad (blue), madder (red) and locally saffron for yellow, which was also used for culinary purposes, an example quoted by G.E. Fussell writing in *The English Countryman:*

Saffron cakes were famous eating, but it was also used to colour 'warden pies', a dainty usual at the sheep shearing festival. Warden pies were made with Warden pears that had been grown originally at the Cistercian Abbey of Warden, Bedfordshire.

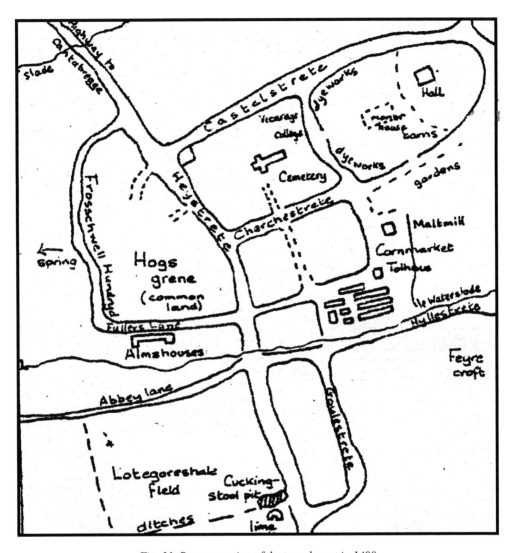

Fig. 31. Reconstruction of the town layout in 1400.

Much has been written about saffron as it was locally of considerable importance being well suited to the chalky soils around Walden and its cultivation extended into Cambridgeshire. Various traditions exist about its introduction, but it is possible it was being grown in the reign of Edward III (1307-77). A century later the crop was well established, sometimes being grown in rotation with teasels which were cultivated for use in the finishing processes during cloth manufacture, fixed into a teasel cross, and used to raise the nap on broadcloth. The teasels grown had hooked spines (*Dipsacus sativus*) unlike the weed form, now found growing on field boundaries, which is a near relative.

Preparation of wool for weaving was in itself an important part of cloth manufacture. After shearing, wool firstly had to be sorted and cleaned, to remove dirt and extraneous matter, after which it passed either to a carder for short wool or to a comber for long. These are two quite different methods of preparing wool for hand spinning. The purpose of carding was to work the wool up into a fluffy mass by means of a pair of hand cards which resembled brushes in shape, the fronts being fitted with short pieces of wire set in a leather and wooden cover (Figs. 32, 33 & 34).

Figs. 32 & 33. A pair of cards (left)' one of a pair of wool combs (right). Fig. 34 below: A 15th century illustration of combing, carding and spinning. Note the wool comb fixed on a post.

The wool was spread in small quantities upon one of the cards and brushed and combed with the other until all the fibres were disentangled, after which it was stripped off the card into soft fleecy rolls called 'batts' or 'rolags'. Most of this work was done by women and children, some of whom also spun yarn. Wool combing used in the preparation of long staple wool is a quite different process which was described in detail in the early 19th century *Book of Trades or Library of Useful Arts*, volume 1. The following is a précis of the article:

Combed wool makes worsted and many kinds of stuff and other articles (worsteds were known as 'stuff' not cloth). The wool is washed in a trough after which the moisture is dried out and drops of oil are added. In each comb there are three, sometimes four, rows of highly tempered steel teeth. Each workman has two combs which he makes hot in a comb-pot that burns charcoal and is shared by four combers. When the combs are hot, he puts on each a certain quantity of wool, free

60

from knots which may impede the operation. He combs the wool from off one comb on to the other alternately until it is exceedingly smooth. He then draws out the fine slivers which are quite long. What is left on the comb is called 'noyle' and is fit only for the manufacture of blankets and coarse cloth. To whiten the wool it is hung in a sealed room with a charcoal fire to which is added powdered brimstone. Vapour from the sulphur must not escape to the open air. Wool combing was carried out usually by a group of men working together in one combing shop. Combing was considered to be a trade injurious to good health due to the fumes from the charcoal pots.

Combing became very important locally and many, many combers were employed in and around Saffron Walden preparing long staple wool for the Norfolk worsted trade some going into Suffolk as well. There was also a little local manufacture (see part 3).

From the 14th and 15th centuries we have some records of local sheep numbers and who owned them. Firstly, there is Dorothy Cromarty's study of the Court Rolls of Chepyng Walden referred to above. The administrative centre of the manor was the house near the decaying Great Hall situated in the outer bailey of Walden Castle. Amongst the buildings there, forming part of the manor farm, was a sheepcote to house the manorial flock in bad weather. Other buildings on the site were two granges (barns), one long house, a house for oxen, one for cows and a stable. Nearby was a barley barn. It would seem that this complex was leased out and that the Great Hall was reserved in the lord's hands. The manorial flock consisted of 200 wether sheep worth two shillings per head and 64 'hoggesters' worth 1s 8d each. Other major landowners, probably leaseholders, had flocks of over 100 and Cromarty gives some figures, viz 300, 240, 160, 300, 240, 300, 200, 160 and 200.

In the late 14th century there were complaints in court that sheep owners were transgressing common grazing rights. These were protected by the stinting rules on all those within the manor and enforced by the manor court in the following way. A verdict explains this:

> The Court of the Manor of Walden by 12 Jurors concerning the common of sheep belonging to the tenants of the whole town. Each tenant in villeinage who holds a virgate [30-39 acres] shall have common of 100 sheep. Those with half-virgates 50, those with 10 acres 30 sheep, those with 6 acres 18 sheep and those with 3 acres 9 sheep.

The final sentence however grants 'tenants at will [free tenants] shall have for every one acre, common for 3 sheep', so a tenant 'at will' with 100 acres could keep 300 sheep on the common grazing but in addition many more on any enclosed land he occupied.[18]

The Abbey at Brook Walden owned sufficient land in their three sheepfolds to accommodate approximately 2,000 sheep making them the largest sheep farmers in the area. Actual numbers kept in the 15th century are not known although a land and rent survey of 1400 gives us some clues from the acreage of the sheepfolds. The Infold near the abbey had 297 acres reserved for ewes and lambs, the Outfold 187 acres for the 'wedder flock' (castrated males kept for their wool), and a further fold at Bolisgrove manor where the abbey had foldage rights and a sheepfold of 170 acres. Bolisgrove lay to the north of the abbey but the site is now part of Westley Farm on Little Walden Road. As the customary stocking rate at the time was three sheep per acre, the total would be nearly 2,000. They had exclusive grazing rights on all manorial lands, the direct tenants of the abbey being forbidden to keep sheep, although other stock were permitted. These would have been mainly draught oxen.[19]

Fleece weights by present-day standards were very low indeed. Most current opinion places them at about 1½-1¾ lb per fleece, with the wethers yielding somewhat more. Twinning was almost unheard of and single lambs were favoured, being generally stronger and their dams more able to suckle a single lamb rather than a pair. Overall the lambing percentage varied between 60% and 90%. Disease control for scab, sometimes treated with sulphur, but normally it was controlled by culling up to three times each year. Liver fluke was common in sheep grazing on low lying damp ground and such grazing was avoided in the autumn when the much feared little white snails were waiting to be eaten and were most numerous. Breeding policy was determined only by the potential for wool production and there is no evidence that animals were bred for mutton or that conformation was considered important. What was important was to ensure that the ewes ran with a ram of good wool potential.[20]

All was about to change with the suppression of the English Monasteries commencing in 1536 and continuing into the following year. On 22 March 1538 the Suffragan Bishop of Colchester surrendered Walden Abbey to Henry VIII and five days later the abbey and its estates were granted to Sir Thomas Audley, Lord Chancellor of England. It is likely that the abbey had decayed and there were only seven monks remaining.

The cloth trade locally continued to supply the needs of the local population and a fulling mill continued to operate at Great Chesterford on the Cam near Ickleton until the mid-17th century. The New Draperies that brought great wealth to other parts of Essex were of little importance to the local area. What was important especially to the local people was woolcombing and spinning linked closely to cloth manufacture outside Essex.

Part 3: The Wool Industry 1538-1770

The following deposition from an enquiry regarding Walden Vicarage, held some years after the dissolution of Walden Abbey and the subsequent granting of the estate and lands to Lord Audley, is of some importance to the study of the sheep and wool industries in the Walden area in the post-Dissolution era:

> And another reason whie the said vicarage is deceased in my Judgement is for about the said sixe and twentie years [more correctly 29/30 years] of King Henrie the eight and since everie Tenant within Walden for everie Acre of free lande might and did keepe three sheepe and for everie Acre of copie two. And the vicar had more tithe [of] wooll and Lambe than he hathe nowe. For after that my Lorde Audley did purchase the Manors and Landes aboute Walden he put the said Tenantes from keeping of sheep so that nowe the vicar hathe no tithe [of] wooll and lambe but of a few sheepe which strange farmers hathe of the Lordes demise who so often shifteth and changeth these sheepe that the vicar hath small tithe of wooll and lambe in their daies. For there is never a one within the town dothe keep Sheepe to his knowledge.[21]

As discussed above, direct tenants of the abbey (Brook Walden manor) had never been allowed to keep sheep but those farming within the town manor did so and the common grazing was subject to stinting rules. Now that Lord Audley owned both manors, he applied the ban on sheep keeping to those living in Chepyng Walden manor as well, which action led to the reduction in the vicar's tithe. There must have been many whose lives were adversely affected by the actions of Lord Audley in contrast to other owners of former ecclesiastical manors, who encouraged all forms of economic activity within their new domains. Lord Audley died in 1544 and this ban on sheep keeping must have been abolished by his successors of the Howard family. Sheep were an essential component in the maintenance of soil fertility in the predominantly mixed/arable farming system of North-west Essex.

Fig. 35. Ram's head carving at Saffron Walden Library.

The deposition confirms that the town manor tenants had previously owned flocks and that now strange farmers, probably drovers, were bringing sheep into Essex. The purpose of this was to supply the expanding London meat market. This constant movement of sheep ('choppeth and changeth') was to be a feature of Essex sheep farms for a long period to come. Sheep from far afield were grazed and possibly sheared before moving to the south Essex marshes, with their plentiful supply of rough grazing before slaughter in London. This points to an early indication of a shift away from pure wool production, where conformation was not considered important, to the 18th century breeding work to improve carcass quality. Because of this movement of sheep into and out of Essex it is difficult to identify an 'Essex sheep type' with certainty.

THE OLD NORFOLK BREED.

Ewe, 3 Years old, the Property of Mr Brown of Narton, descended from the flock of Mr Turner of Cenle the Lamb, a cross with the Southdown

PROFESSOR LOW'S ILLUSTRATIONS OF THE BREEDS OF THE DOMESTIC ANIMALS.

Published February 1842, by Longman, Orme, Brown, Green & Longmans, Paternoster Row London

Fig. 36. A ewe of the Norfolk breed with her hornless Southdown cross lamb.

If on entering the Saffron Walden Library, which was formerly the Corn Exchange (the corn market), you were to look up just above the main door you would see the head of a horned ram included there as a reminder of the importance of the wool trade in former times (Fig. 35). The Corn Exchange was built in 1848 on the site of the Woolstaplers' Hall. This head is clearly that of a Norfolk Horn Ram (Fig 36 – see also Fig. 23), a breed of sheep which were kept throughout East Anglia for their fine short-staple wool.

It is one of three types identified by Robert Trow-Smith as being commonly kept in Essex. The other two were a long-woolled coarse type, probably originally derived from Kentish marsh stock and around Epping a fine woolled type similar to some south-western breeds. These two breeds were probably of lesser importance in North-west Essex than the Norfolk Horn. Paintings and images of the 17th century show they were to be found also in Cambridgeshire, and the Audley End Home Farm had a flock in the 18th century according to Arthur Young.

These Norfolk black-faced sheep had origins in central Asia where they roamed on the extensive plains and were thus well adapted to the heathlands of Norfolk and Suffolk. They were less happy in the confines of the arable fold course system where their impatient wanderings were restricted. However, despite these demerits they were held in high repute by many farmers for their fleeces of fine short wool and when on good pasture they 'fleshed up' quickly. These characteristics were to become more important as the demands for mutton increased, at the same time as the East Anglian wool trade faltered and declined in the late 18th century. These pure-bred Norfolks were crossed with the Southdown to produce the Suffolk, today one of the commonest black-faced, hornless sheep on British farms. In the 19th century pure bred Norfolks became increasingly unpopular and eventually nearly died out as a pure breed.

Some few of the last of this breed were kept at Howe Hall, Littlebury Green in 1954 by Mr Bill Harvey before being transferred to Whipsnade, where they remained for the next 12 years. Today they are recognized by the Rare Breed Survival Trust and their numbers have once again increased. Locally a large flock is today kept at Kentwell Hall, Long Melford, and there are several more flocks on rare-breed farms.[22]

Sheep continued to be folded in the time-honoured way within wattle-hurdled enclosures on the fallows to clean and manure the ground. While a mix of arable/livestock farming prevailed in North-west Essex, a departure from traditional methods slowly emerged. Manorial lords in a move to avoid paying costly wages for work on their large arable farms, formerly carried out by customary labour which cost little or nothing, put more of their land down to enclosed grass sheepwalks and employed only a shepherd, but few other workers. Records of these sheepwalks exist in Newport and an extensive sheepwalk at Langley was occupied by a Thaxted man Thomas Sawarde in 1588.[23] On the Audley End Estate there were sheepwalks in 1600 north of Saffron Walden named Burne, Manol and Westley and to the east another named Buckenhoe, all examples of Tudor enclosures. A substantial acreage of pasture existed also in 1600 at the secondary manors of Butlers and St Aylotts.[24]

Although wool is mentioned only rarely in wills, one from Radwinter dated 1569 bequeaths to his wife '20 lbs of my sheep wool to be delivered to my wife yearly and 8 lb of old wool'. In another from Radwinter of the same date, Thomas Wackefielde, husbandman left 'all wool in my house to be equally divided between my wife Joan and my daughter and Anne Coote my daughter-in-law'.

Finally from Littlebury it is recorded that John Ferrer 'unjustly commoned and depastured his sheep in the common ways and fields of the manor... to the injury of the tenants'. He also beat the children and servants of three tenants in resenting it.[25]

The textile industry in and around Saffron Walden in the 18th century had a quite separate history from the rest of Essex as it lay outside the western boundary of the limits of the baye and saye trade, according to Arthur Brown.[26] Its importance, leaving aside any local manufacture, lay in woolcombing and spinning fine yarn for the Norfolk and Suffolk based worsted trade. There were some 6,000 looms at one time working in Norwich alone, each requiring up to ten hand spinners to supply sufficient yarn. Worsted could only be woven with yarn made from long-staple wool in both the warp and weft. Essex imported long-staple wool from Kent, Sussex, Buckinghamshire, Oxfordshire, the Midlands and Lincolnshire. It was brought into Essex by road, river and sea, Lincolnshire and the Midlands being the most likely source of supply for North-west Essex.[27]

Wool combing attracted combers from other parts of the country who moved into North-west Essex. Because of the availability of fine yarn, a small amount of worsted was woven locally. One business at Rickling both spun and wove worsted and one in Saffron Walden, J.D. Archer, continued to do so until at least 1823. Thomas Fuller of Audley End owned a stock worth £3,657. The Burroughs family of Great Sampford were involved in the worsted trade and later operated from Haverhill.[28]

Figs. 37 & 38. Two images of Bishop Blaize: left, from a West Country trade token; below, from the Spring family parclose in the parish church of St Peter & St Paul, Lavenham.

So important was woolcombing in North-west Essex that the feast day of St Blaize was commemorated every year on 3 February. 'Bishop Blaize' was the patron saint of the woolcombers (Figs. 37 & 38). John Player, writing in his *Sketches of Saffron Walden* in 1845, describes the annual procession which visited Newport and Littlebury having passed by Audley End. Included in the throng were the Mayor and Corporation and a band to provide much music. The procession was headed by the 'bishop', shepherds and shepherdesses, the latter carrying a lamb. On return to Walden the assembled company dined at The Rose and the church bells were rung. The last procession, it is thought, was held in 1778 some years after dark clouds had gathered over the whole of the Essex woollen textile industry.[29]

By 1740 the cloth industry in Essex was beginning a terminal decline but hung on for many more years. Agriculture in Essex was turning more to intensive arable farming to supply an expanding London food market and a greater demand for meat including mutton. The East Anglian cloth industry was losing its importance as new centres in the north were developed, where large mills on fast-flowing streams could be built and long-staple wool was available nearby.

War destroyed the trade routes to Spain used by the 'Baye trade' in Essex to supply their principle export market. Joseph Savill of Braintree wrote in 1788 that 'his spinners had not half the work to do' because Spain and France were at war: 'I now have more than 1050 Bays and no prospects of selling them. Wool has never been cheaper or the trade worse.'[30]

As the trade in wool declined so the malting industry in and around Saffron Walden expanded its investment and output in response to higher demand from the London brewers, but only employed relatively few people. During the Napoleonic wars farmers expanded their cereal production in response to wartime shortages and higher prices. The decline in wool combing and especially spinning led to considerable distress and unrest amongst the landless classes. In 1813 boys and girls in Clavering could be hired for spinning at one penny per pound of wool spun.[31]

However, let me end on a more cheerful note with two verses about happier times for the wool industry written by Thomas Tusser, the Essex-born poet and agricultural sage. Born at Rivenhall in the 16th century and educated in London and Cambridge, he later farmed at Brantham in Suffolk.

> Wash sheep for the better, where water doth run,
> And let him go cleanly and lay in the sun.
> Then shear him – quite closely, at two days end
> For sooner the better, his corps will amend.
>
> Reward not thy sheep when ye take off his coat
> With cuts and raw patches as broad as a groat!
> Let no such ungentleness happen to thine,
> Lest fly lay her eggs there and make poor sheep pine!

The illustration in Fig. 39 has been included as it shows the numerous trades involved in the production of cloth, starting with the farmer who kept the sheep, through to the 'saylor' who carried the final product, fine English cloth, to distant export markets. It emphasizes the importance not only of the cloth trade to those employed in it, but as the major source of British revenue for many centuries.

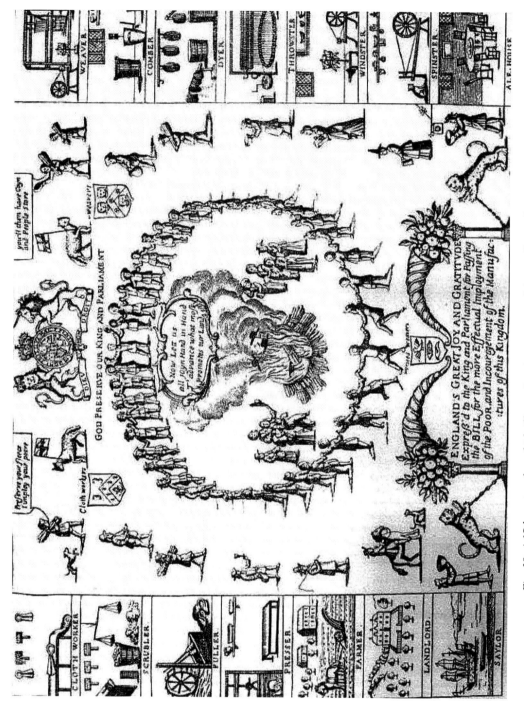

Fig. 39. A 17th century broadside illustrating the processes of the woollen and worsted industries.

Postscript

Looking back over the last 40 years the people of Saffron Walden have seen numerous changes to their town. Most of the farming services which previously were very prominent in the town have now gone and any direct connection to the farming world no longer exists.

Back in 1969 the weekly auction sales of cattle, pigs and poultry continued to flourish, bringing farmers, transporters and drovers into the town centre, creating a sense of occasion (Fig. 40). Market Day really meant something special. While the Corn Exchange had recently closed down, the town still retained the offices of two agricultural merchants, both now gone, and several more from nearby towns operated in this area. Three machinery companies had premises in the town providing servicing facilities, tractors and implements.

Outside Saffron Walden, Chesterford Park Agricultural Research Station, owned by Fisons, was well-established and highly regarded. Ciba Geigy had trial grounds at Whittlesford. The Farmers Fertiliser Company still manufactured fertilisers at Royston, supplying many local farmers. And at Audley End cattle grazed in the park where people now walk their dogs and 'take the air'. All these activities contributed to a feeling that Saffron Walden was indeed a market town that was responding to the needs of the farming industry – it was a farming centre.

Does it matter that the town has changed? All the facilities and services once centred in the town are still available at other places and in other forms - grain and livestock are still bought and sold and farm machinery is still available, research is still carried out, if on a much lesser scale by fewer people. So is there a problem?

Two recent thought-provoking quotations highlight causes for concern:

> Fewer people encounter farming in their everyday lives than ever before, and there are many layers of shrink-wrap between people and their food. That means we need to spend a lot more time teasing out the truth.

(Tom Oliver, Director of Rural Policy for the Campaign to Protect Rural England)

> Unlike the French, where every townsperson has an uncle or cousin on a farm, we have lost our tribal memory of the countryside. It now seems that a fifth of children grow up without ever visiting it.

(Clive Aslet, Editor at Large of *Country Life*)

Day-to-day farming activities have become remote to 'the man in the street'. He knows it goes on but sees less of it in his everyday busy life – does this matter? The problem seems to arise firstly from that very remoteness of farming today and there is probably a greater need for clarity. Secondly, nationally farming is now given a lower priority than previously in the affairs of the country. This must be a cause of concern in a world that is uncertain of its future sufficiency of food to feed our expanding population.

Land Agriculture and Industry

Fig. 40. Scenes from the last day of Saffron Walden cattle market on 15 December 1981.

Clockwise from top left: cattle unloading; Alan Rust (left) who drove away the last truck-load of livestock; Mike Hamilton, Claude Hockley and others in the auction ring; farmers in the empty yard; David Magness of Lodge Farm, Thaxted, winner of the last cup awarded; George Martin and Paul Goodman with John Whittaker of Cheffins.

Spotlights on a Land Remembered

Fig. 41. Threshing and chaff cutting at New House Farm, Ashdon in 1924.

This remarkable photograph highlights a rural world now gone forever, but once a typical scene on the farms of North-west Essex. The photograph comes from the collection of Gordon Ridgewell who worked at New House Farm, Ashdon as a lad. The horse-keeper, shown beside the horse, was his grandfather, Robert Ridgewell who started work at 6.30 a.m., walking two miles from Radwinter, then another 10-12 miles each day with his horses. His son Joseph, pictured beside the wheel of the cart, worked there all his life. Also in the photograph are Harry Hutching and Bill Hutching in front of the threshing engine. In 1951 the Hutchings bought their first combine harvester, a Massy Harris costing £1,080 - it was to be the beginning of another agricultural revolution.

REFERENCES

1: Local Farming in a Bygone Age

1. The Steward of the Manors in 1758 was a John Craster and his deputy was Thomas Butler (information from L. Barker).
2. Titow, J.Z., *English Rural Society 1200-1350* (1969), p. 9.
3. Audley End Farm Maps 1758 at ERO: St Aylotts D/DQy 13 (Grid Ref 569399); Butlers D/DQy 12 (GR 560407); Westley D/DU 120 (GR 532402); Ross D/Dby D/Dqy 11 (548361); Pounce Hall T/M 124 (GR 563383); Monks Hall D/DQy 14 (GR 559431); Audley End T/M 123 (GR 525377).
4. Arthur Young, Secretary of the Board of Agriculture from 1793, died 1820: *Agriculture of Essex*, 1807.
5. ERO D/Dby 9: 1 January 1747, Little Walden Park.
6. ERO D/Dby 9: 1 January 1747 Catmer Hall, Littlebury.

2: Home Farm at Audley End

1. ERO D/D By A262-270 Audley End Monthly Farm Accounts, 9 vols 1772-1888. The Home Farm accounts are complete for the years 1772-1888. They are contained in a series of green leather-bound volumes beautifully written up, month by month showing every transaction that took place for 'Disbursements' and 'Sales' covering two pages with a balance drawn at the foot of the page. They are indeed a remarkable record, not unique, but certainly unusual, extremely detailed and valuable.
2. ERO D/D By A268: 1851 Home Farm Accounts.
3. ERO D/D By A265: January & July1811 Home Farm Accounts.
4. *The Jersey Cow a Darling of the World*, The Jersey Cattle Society of the United Kingdom.
5. Thornton, J., *English Herd Book of Jersey Cattle,* vol 1 (1879), p. 68.
6. Saffron Walden Museum 41359: Catalogue of a Dispersal Sale of the entire Audley End Jersey herd and flock of Southdown Sheep.
7. Young, A., *Agriculture of Essex* (1807).

3: Horham Hall, Thaxted

1. Rush, J.A., *Seats in Essex* (1897), p. 107: Horham Hall *c.*1916 (Saffron Walden Town Library).
2. ERO d/P 19/1/2. Broxted Parish Records – Burial 26 August 1807.
3. ERO Wills 387 MR 13: Mary But(t)le, Broxted.
4. ERO 35/1/1-45 Horham Hall 35/1/14. These two references are but a small part of a very large collection of the working papers of 18th and 19th century Thaxted valuers, auctioneers, land agents and surveyors held in the ERO (Acc. 4911A D/F 35). The collection is fully described in the introductory notes. With thanks to Mr L. Barker for pointing these out to me.
5. Essex Wills 181 MR 12: 1763, Robert Buttle, Broxted.
6. Essex Wills 398 MR 12: 1774, Susanna Buttle.
7. Essex Wills 387 MR 13: 1807, Mary Butle, Broxted.
8. Vancouver, C. *General View of the Agriculture in Essex* (1795), p. 97.
9. Young, A. *General View of Agriculture of Essex (1807)*.
10. Young, *op, cit.*, p. 150 – the Shim is illustrated in Plate XXVII.
11. ERO D/DSh/P3: A Survey of the several Estates in the County of Essex belonging to Charles Smyth Esq as taken in 1749 by T. Skynner.

4: Mitchells Farm at Little Walden

1. Monteith, D., *Saffron Walden and its Environs* (MA thesis, unpub. 1958), p. 158.
2. PRO. C66/679: *Extract of Letters and Papers Foreign & Domestic of Henry VIII*, 1538 – Grants July.
3. Rackham, O., *The History of the Countryside* (1986), p. 5.
4. See note 2.
5. ERO D/Dby T4/599.
6. The Field Book of Walden 1758 (Saffron Walden Town Library).
7. *op. cit.*, p. 36.
8. ERO D/DU 1/107, will of Charles Parris.
9. ERO D/Dby/A299: 'Previous to the division of the Estate, Wm Whitwell Esq. & the Honourable Ann Whitwell his wife, Book of Farming Accounts'.
10. ERO D/Dby/E9: Little Walden Park: report on the farm by Thomas Pennystone, Land Steward.
11. ERO D/P 18/3/102L: Notebook of the tithe valuation written by Rev J. North c.1792-1810 for Mitchells farm in Ashdon parish.
12. Hunt, E.H., & Parris, S.J., 'Essex Agriculture in the Golden Age', *Agricultural History Review*, vol 43, part II (1995), p. 162.
13. Brown, R.J., *English Farmhouses* (1993), p. 108.

5: The Floor Malting Industry

PART 1

1. Mathias, P., *The Brewing Industry in England 1700-1830* (1959), p. 389.
2. Mingay, G..E., *The Agricultural Revolution 1650-1800* (1977), p. 202.
3. Steer F.W., *Farm & Cottage Inventories of Mid-Essex 1635-1749* (1950), p. 32.
4. Brown, A.F.J., *Essex at Work 1700-1815* (1969), p. 60.
5. Cobbett W., *Cottage Economy 1821-1822* (1926 edition, Oxford 1979), p. 19.
6. Defoe D., *A Tour through the Whole of England 1724*, pp. 118-9.
7. Overton M.. *Agricultural Revolution in England* (1996), p. 107.
8. Mathias, *op.cit.*, p. 463.
9. Moore H.I., *Background to Farming* (1947), p. 20.
10. Mathias, *op.cit.*, p. 463.
11. Stopes H., 'Malt & Malting', Lyon, F.W., *The Brewers Journal* 1885: Malting post-1300.
12. Mathias, *op.cit.*, p. 355.
13. Clark C., *The British Malting Industry Since 1830* (1998), p. 25.
14. Mathias, *op cit.*, pp. 12-21.
15. *op.cit.*, pp. 469-70.
16. *op.cit.*, p. 470.
17. *op.cit.*, p. 460.
18. *op.cit.*, p. 461.
19. *op.cit.*, p. 375.
20. *op cit.*, p. 418.
21. Clark, *op. cit.*, p. 15.
22. *op cit.*, p. 36.
23. Paye, P., *The Saffron Walden Branch Line* (1981).
24. Clark, *op.cit.*, Appendix 1.

PART 2

25. Mathias, *op.cit.*, p. 408.
26. Clark, *op.cit.*, p. 8.
27. Mathias, *op.cit.* p. 377.
28. Crosby, T., 'The development of malthouses around the Herts-Essex border', *Industrial Archaeology Review* XXII: 1 2000, p. 45.
29. Stopes, H., 'Malt and malting' in Lyon, F.W., *The Brewers Journal* 1885. Malting post-1300.
30. Richardson, S., *High Street Maltings, Saffron Walden Historic Building Record* (1998), p. 6.
31. Peaty, I.P., *Essex Brewers: the malting and hop industry of the county* (1992), p. 128.
32. ERO D/DBy E17.
33. Crosby, *op.cit.*, p. 33.
34. Saffron Walden Museum 40017.
35. Addison, W., *Audley End* (1953), p. 169.
36. Boyes, J. & Roland, R., *The Canals of Eastern England* (1977), p. 46.
37. Clark, *op.cit.*, pp. 65-8.
38. Perren, R., *Agriculture in Depression* (1995), p. 9.
39. Clark, *op.cit.*, Appendix 3, p. 251.
40. *op.cit.*, pp. 36-8.

6: A Canal for Saffron Walden?

1. Maps of these three proposals are held in the ERO under the following references. I am grateful to Mr L. Barker for providing details of them:
(a) 1777/80 – D/D By/P3/2: Map of 'proposed navigable canal from Bishop's Stortford to Cambridge: Surveyed by order of the City of London in 1779 and 1780 by Robert Whitworth, Engineer. Engraved by Wm Faden' (London and Cambridge junction Canal, Bishop's Stortford to Cambridge) 1½ ins to 1 mile, 8 ins by 37 ins. Course runs close to river Stort to Elsenham, thence after a tunnel close to river Cam near to Audley End thence close to the Cam towards Cambridge.
(b) 1789/90 – D/D By/P4: Fully described in the text.
(c) 1811/12 - D/D By/P3/1: Map of intended London and Cambridge Junction canal, Bishop's Stortford to Cambridge. Ralph Walker, Engineer (original signature) 1½ ins to 1 mile, 11ins by 41 ins. Course runs close to the river Stort to Elsenham, thence after a tunnel close to the river Cam to near Audley End, whence a detour through two tunnels between the park and Saffron Walden town thence close to the Cam towards Cambridge.
2. Boucher, C.T.G., *John Rennie 1761-1812* (1963).
3. My thanks are due to Zofia Everett of the ERO Archive Access Point in Saffron Walden, who put me in touch with the owner of an original engraving of map (b) which he had purchased at an auction.

7: The Wool Industry of North-west Essex

PART 1

1. Waugh, S., *England in the Reign of Edward III* (1991).
2. Heard, N., *Wool in East Anglia – The Golden Fleece* (1970).
3. Darby, H. C., *The Domesday Geography of Eastern England* (1952), pp. 209-63.
4. Lamond, E., *Walter of Henley: Husbandry & Seneschaucie* (1890).
5. Trow-Smith, R., *A History of British Livestock Husbandry to 1700*, Vol 1 (1957).
6. Cromarty, D., *The Fields of Saffron Walden in 1400* (1966).
7. *The Abbey of Tilty* (information at parish church).

8. Hunter, J., *Field Systems in Essex* (2003).
9. Miller, E., *The Abbey and Bishopric of Ely* (1969).
10. Williamson, G., *Information from the 1251 Survey of Episcopal Lands of Littlebury* (2005).
11. Miller, E. & Hatcher, J., *Medieval England 1086-1348* (1978).

PART 2

12. Waugh, S., *England in the Reign of Edward III* (1991).
13. Williamson, G., Notification of a Quit Claim 1321 and notification of a grant 1334 both in Littlebury.
14. McCann, J., *Agrarian Change and the Cloth Industry in Essex 1350-1500.* (PhD thesis unpub., 1970: ERO T/Z 75/19).
15. Lipson, E., *A History of the English Woollen and Worsted Industries* (1921); *The Economic History of England* Vol 1 (1959).
16. Everett, M. *The Lost Buildings of Saffron Walden* (2001), pp. 30-33.
17. Cromarty, D. *Chepyng Walden 1381-1420: a study from the Court Rolls* (1967). *Essex Journal* II (1967).
18. Emson, C.H., Transcript copy of the Cartulary 1387, Verdict taken in the court of the manor of Walden concerning the common of sheep belonging to the tenants of the whole town. British Museum Harleian MS3697.
19. Cromarty, D., *The Fields of Saffron Walden in 1400* (1966).
20. Trow-Smith, R., *A History of British Livestock Husbandry to 1700* (1957).

PART 3

21. Hull, F., *Agriculture and Rural Society in Essex 1560-1640* (unpub. PhD thesis, London 1950: ERO D/DBy T9/3).
22. Trow-Smith, R., *British Livestock Husbandry to 1700* (1957); Wade-Martins, P., *Black Faces: a history of East Anglian sheep breeds* (1993).
23. Emmison, F.G., *Elizabethan Life: home, work and land* (1991).
24. Monteith, D., *Saffron Walden and its Environs* (unpub. MA thesis, 1958).
25. Emmison, *op.cit.*
26. Brown, A.F.J., *Essex at Work* (1969).
27. Burley, K.H., *The Economic Development of Essex in the later 17th and early 18th Centuries* (unpub. PhD thesis, 1957).
28. Brown, *op.cit.*; Curtis, G., *The Story of the Sampfords* (1981).
29. *Victoria County History of Essex*, Vol 2, pp. 308-404.
30. Quoted in exhibit at Braintree Museum 2006.
31. Ludgate, E. M., *Clavering & Langley 1783-1983* (1984), p. 32.

See also Carter, T., 'Treasures at Caton Lane' *Saffron Walden Historical Journal*, No 1, Spring 2001, describing a metal detector survey in which 26 cloth seals of 16-17th date were discovered on the Catons Lane football club site – it was thought this may have been the site of a cloth fair, linked to the work of dyers, clothiers and alnagers.

Bibliography

Primary Sources

Essex Record Office
ERO D/Dby 9: A262-270 Audley End Monthly Farm Accounts, 1772-1888
D/Dby/A299: Whitwell 'Book of Farming Accounts'
Wills: 387 MR 13; 35/1/14; 181 MR 12; 398 MR 12; D/DU 1/109
D/DQy: Audley End Farm Maps 1758: St Aylotts D/DQy 13; Butlers D/DQy 12; Westley D/DU 120; Ross D/Dqy 11; Pounce Hall T/M 124; Monks Hall D/DQy 14; Audley End T/M 123; D/Dby/E9: Little Walden Park; D/DBy E17;
D/D By/P3/1-3: Canal maps 1769-1812
D/Dby T4/599: Deeds of Manor or Ashdon Hall 1724-95
D/DBy T9/3: Deeds Miscellaneous 1564-1842
D/Dby/E9: Little Walden Park (Audley End Estate, Particulars of Estate 1748)
D/DSh/P3: A Survey of several Estates in the County of Essex belonging to Charles Smyth Esq as taken in 1749 by T. Skynner
D/P 18/3/102: Mitchells Farm valuation, *c.*1792-1810, Vol No 5, 'Notebook of tithe valuations written by Rev J. North *c.*1792-1810 for Mitchells Farm in Ashdon parish'.
Braintree Museum: Exhibit 2006: quotation by Joseph Savill of Braintree, 1788.
Saffron Walden Museum: SWM 40017: Annual movement from Walden to Bishops Stortford of barley & malt, 1788; SWM 41359: Catalogue of a Dispersal Sale of the entire Audley End Jersey herd & flock of Southdown Sheep.
Saffron Walden Town Library: The Field Book of Walden, 1758
Emson, C.H., Transcript copy of the Cartulary. 1387, Verdict taken ion the court of the manor of Walden concerning the common of sheep belonging to the tenants of the whole town.
Monteith, D., *Saffron Walden and its Environs* (unpub. MA thesis, 1958)
Rush, J. H., *Seats in Essex* (1897), p.107: Horham Hall c.1916.
The National Archives: PRO C66/679: Grants, 1538.
The British Museum Harleian MS3697
Other sources: *The Abbey of Tilty* (information at parish church)
The Jersey Cow - a darling of the world, The Jersey Cattle Society of the United Kingdom (website)

Secondary Sources

Addison, William *Audley End* (J. M. Dent & Sons, 1953)
Boucher, C.T.G. *John Rennie 1761-1812* (Manchester University Press, 1963)
Boyes, J. & Roland, R., *The Canals of Eastern England* (David & Charles, 1977)
Brown, A.F.J., *Essex at Work 1700-1815* (Essex Record Office, 1969)
Brown, R.J., *English Farmhouses* (Robert Hale Ltd, 1992)
Burley, K.H., *The Economic Development of Essex in the later 17th and early 18th Centuries* (unpub. PhD thesis, 1957 at ERO)
Carter, T., 'Treasures at Caton Lane', *Saffron Walden Historical Journal*, No 1 (2001)
Clark C., *The British Malting Industry Since 1830* (Hambledon Press, 1998)
Cobbett, W., *Cottage Economy 1821-1822* (1926 edition, Oxford 1979)
Cromarty, D. 'Chepyng Walden 1381-1420: a study from the Court Rolls' in *Essex Journal* II (1967)
Cromarty, D. *The Fields of Saffron Walden in 1400* (ERO Publications No 43, 1966)
Crosby, T., 'The development of malthouses around the Herts-Essex border' in *Industrial Archaeology Review* XXII: 1 (2000)
Curtis, G., *The Story of the Sampfords* (Self-published,1981)
Darby, H.C. *The Domesday Geography of Eastern England* (Cambridge University Press, 1952)

Defoe, D., *A Tour through the Whole of England* (1724)

Emmison, F.G., *Elizabethan Life: home, work and land* (Essex Record Office, 1991)

Everett, M. *The Lost Buildings of Saffron Walden* (Harts, 2001).

Fussell, G. E. & K.R., *The English Countryman: from Tudor times to the Victorian Age* (Bloomsbury Books, 1981)

Hartley, D. & Elliot, M.M., *Life & Work of the People of England* (B.T. Batsford, 1931)

Heard, N., *Wool in East Anglia – The Golden Fleece* (Terence Dalton Ltd, 1970).

Hull, F. *Agriculture and Rural Society in Essex 1560-1640* (unpub. PhD thesis, London 1950 in ERO).

Hunt, E. H. & Parris, S. J., 'Essex Agriculture in the Golden Age', *Agricultural History Review*, vol 43, part II (1995).

Hunter, J., *Field Systems in Essex* (Essex Society for Archaeology & History, 2003).

Hurley, B. (ed.), *The Book of Trades or Library of Useful Arts,* vol 1 (1811) Reprint Wiltshire Family History Society.

Lamond, E., *Walter of Henley: Husbandry & Seneshaucie* (Longmans Green & Co, 1890).

Lipson, E. *The History of the English Woollen & Worsted Industries* (A & C Black, 1921).

Lipson, E., *The Economic History of England* Vol 1 (Adam & Charles Black, 1915, 12th ed. 1959).

Ludgate, E. M., *Clavering & Langley 1783-1983* (Self-published, 1984).

Mathias, P., *The Brewing Industry in England 1700-1830* (CUP, 1959).

McCann, J. *Agrarian Change and the Cloth Industry in Essex 1350-1500* (PhD thesis, unpub., 1970, in ERO T/Z 75/19).

Miller, E. & Hatcher, J. *Medieval England 1086-1348* (Longman Group, 1978).

Miller, E., *The Abbey and Bishopric of Ely* (CUP 1951, 2nd ed. 1969).

Mingay, G..E., *The Agricultural Revolution 1650-1800* (Adams & Chas Black, 1977).

Moore, H. I., *Background to Farming* (Geo Allen & Unwin Ltd., 1947).

Overton, M., *Agricultural Revolution in England* (CUP, 1996).

Paye, P., *The Saffron Walden Branch Line* (Oxford Pub. Co., 1981).

Peaty, I.P.., *Essex Brewers: the malting and hop industry of the county* (The Brewery Society Publications, 1992).

Perren, R. *Agriculture in Depression* (CUP, 1995).

Player, J., *Sketches of Saffron Walden* (1845).

Pyne, W.H., *Rustic Vignettes for Artists and Craftsmen* (1824) – reprint by Dover Publications, New York (1977).

Rackham, O., *The History of the Countryside* (J.M. Dent & Sons, 1986).

Richardson, S., *High Street Maltings, Saffron Walden Historic Building Record* (AOC Archaeology, 1998).

Saffron Walden History (Old Series, Saffron Walden Historical Society) Nos 3 (1973), 9 (1976), 13 (1978) & 29 (1986).

Steer, F.W., *Farm and Cottage Inventories of Mid-Essex 1635-1749* (Essex Record Office, 1956).

Stopes, H., 'Malt & Malting' in Lyon, F.W., *The Brewers Journal* (1885).

Thornton, J., *English Herd Book of Jersey Cattle*, vol 1 (1879).

Titow, J. Z. *English Rural Society 1200-1350* (George Allen & Unwin, 1969).

Trow –Smith, R. A *History of British Livestock Husbandry to 1700*, Vol 1 (Routledge & Kegan Paul, 1957).

Tusser, T., 'Junes Husbandrie', from *Five Hundred Points of Good Husbandry*, (1524-80), Ch.42 (OUP, 1984).

Vancouver, C., *General View of the Agriculture in Essex* (1795).

Victoria County History of Essex, Vol 2 (1907).

Wade-Martins, P., *Black Faces: a history of East Anglian sheep breeds* (Norfolk Museum Service in assoc. with 'Geering of Ashford', 1993).

Waugh, S.L., *England in the Reign of Edward III* (CUP, 1991).

Williamson, G. Notification of a Quit Claim 1321 and notification of a grant 1334 both in Littlebury.

Williamson, G., *Information from the 1251 Survey of Episcopal Lands of Littlebury* (2005).

Young, A., *General View of the Agriculture of Essex* (1807).

INDEX

(SW) = Saffron Walden

Hartlib, S., 29
Harlow, 14, 41
Harlow Bush Fairs, 7
Harvey, Bill, 65
Haverhill, 65
Hayward, John, 16
Hempstead, 13
Henry Doubleday Research Association, 5, 8
Hertford, 31
Hertfordshire, 25, 27-32, 35-36, 41, 53
Hervey, Lord, 3
High Easter, 57
High Street (SW), 26, 30, 38, 40-41, 43
Hill Street (SW), 40
Hinckford Hundred, 50
Hinxton, 44
Hockerill Highway, 41
Hockley, Claude, 70
Horham Hall, 11-16
Horsefrith Park, 37
Howard family, 63
Howe Hall, Littlebury Green, 65
Hundreds, 50, 57
Hunter, John, 53, 55
Huntingdon, 31
Hutching, Bill & Harry, 71

Ickleton, 62
India, 42
Industrial Revolution, 25
Ipswich, 49
Italy, 53, 57

Kent, 17, 65
Kentwell Hall, 65
Kings
   Edward I, 49
   Edward II, 49
   Edward III, 49, 55, 59
   Henry VII, 57
   Henry VIII, 57, 62
   John, 57
King Street (SW), 57
King, Gregory, 25
King, Martha, 21
King, Sarah, 18
Kings Lynn, 44, 49

Lakenheath Lode, 44
Langley, 65
Lavenham, 66
Lee Navigation, 28, 31
Library (SW), 63-64
Lincolnshire, 30, 43, 65
Linton, 18, 44
Lt Abington, 44
Lt Chesterford, 38, 44
Lt Henham, 44
Lt Walden,18-19, 21-22, 41
Lt Walden Airfield, 24
Lt Walden Park, 20-21, 24
Lt Walden Road (SW), 61
Littlebury, 44, 53-54, 57, 65-66
Littlebury Green, 48, 53, 64
Livestock, 4-5, 10, 16, 20-21, 25, 28-29, 50
   Alderney cattle, 6-7
   cattle, 4, 5-7, 9-10, 12-14, 20, 22, 69
   horses, 16, 42
   Jersey cattle, 6
   Kentish marsh sheep, 61
   Long Horned Derby cattle, 13-14
   Merino sheep, 7
   Norfolk Horn sheep, 8, 48, 64-65
   oxen, 2, 18, 53, 61
   pigs, 14, 20, 69
   plough horses, 18
   poultry, 5, 69
   sheep, 4, 7-8, 16, 20-21, 29, 48-49, 61-63
   Shorthorn cattle, 6
   Soay sheep, 51
   Southdown sheep, 7, 9, 64-65
   Suffolk Punches, 6
   Suffolk sheep, 65
   Suffolk cattle, 14
   Yorkshire polled cattle, 6
   – see also wool industry
Lodge farm, Thaxted, 70
London, 13, 27-28, 31-32, 36, 41-42, 44, 55, 57, 63, 66-67, 69
Long Melford, 65
Lord Chancellor, 62
Lord Inchcape, 263
Lord Howard – see Braybrooke
Lower Square (SW), 40